Cooking for Your Hyperactive Child

Cooking for Your Hyperactive Child

Foreword by Kenneth Krischer, M.D., Ph.D.

June Roth

cbi **Contemporary Books, Inc.**
Chicago

Published by Contemporary Books, Inc.
180 North Michigan Avenue, Chicago, Illinois 60601
Manufactured in the United States of America
Library of Congress Catalog Card Number: 77-75849
International Standard Book Number: 0-8092-7832-4 (cloth)
0-8092-7408-6 (paper)

Published simultaneously in Canada by
Beaverbooks
953 Dillingham Road
Pickering, Ontario L1W 1Z7
Canada

To Theron Randolph, M.D., for his remarkable insight into the relationship between allergies and behavior problems, and for his persistence over the past three decades in bringing this awareness to the medical community.

Contents

Foreword

At last a cookbook I can refer anxious parents to for help with special diets to control their child's behavior. At last a cookbook for the family that recognizes that hyperactivity is a family problem. At last a cookbook that demonstrates that a diet free of "junk foods" can be nutritious and appealing.

Over the past years I have seen hundreds of children who were previously diagnosed as hyperactive or autistic, learning disabled, emotionally disturbed, or as having minimum brain dysfunction. Many were on medications, such as tranquilizers, sedatives, stimulants, or antidepressants. As we investigated these problems, it became more and more evident that the cause was a sensitivity to foods or food additives. What a delight to the parent and physician to see a child who was the class disrupter or "cut up" transformed to a calm "solid citizen" merely by the removal of a few foods or additives, such as milk, chocolate, wheat, and food colors, from his diet.

Hyperactive behavior in children due to food sensitivity was first described by Dr. Theron Randolph in 1947. Since then many investigators, such as Dr. A. H. Rowe, Dr. Frederick Speer, Dr. Stephen Lockey, and Dr. Ben Feingold have elaborated and explained these relationships. Yet, children are daily being placed on drugs to control their hyperactive behavior or short attention span. After thirty years we are still treating symptoms even though the causes have been described.

June Roth also recognizes that the solution begins in the supermarket. We have to begin to read labels and recognize that offending foods may show up in the least expected places. For example, it is always amazing to my patients to find out how many foods contain corn or corn products. It can be found even on a postage stamp!

Included in this book is a list of some of the common offending food additives. It is estimated there are over 1,600 additives currently in our foods. Which of these may have long-term adverse biological effects is not known. We must demand and encourage more research on the effects of these additives. It is significant that many food colors have been removed from the market after previously having been approved as safe.

June Roth's *pièce de résistance* is a quick picture index for each recipe, which enables readers to see at a glance which recipes fulfill their child's particular dietary requirements. I have the feeling that many mothers forced to get away from prepared and convenience foods will rediscover the pleasures of creating in the kitchen.

This book then is an epoch in many ways. However, it should be only a beginning; as we find more and more offending additives and foods we can look forward to many more June Roth cookbooks in the future.

Kenneth N. Krischer, Ph.D., M.D.

Dear Reader:

I have written many kinds of specialized cookbooks with particular medical problems in mind. None has gripped me as tightly as this research to help the hyperactive child and family. It has involved traveling all over our country to speak to leading doctors who work in this field, with the hope that a simple talk from my kitchen to yours would bring you the latest thinking on the subject.

While studies are going on, children are growing up. The information in this book therefore is not conclusive but merely a reflection of what pioneering doctors are prescribing at this time to try to ease the activity of the hyperactive child through changes in diet.

My grateful thanks for giving me valuable time and information go, in alphabetical order, to Dr. Allan Cott of New York City, New York; Dr. Ben F. Feingold of San Francisco, California; Dr. Kenneth Krischer of the Florida Institute of Neuro-Dynamics, Plantation, Florida; Dr. Marshall Mandell of the New England Foundation for Allergic and Environmental Diseases, Norwalk, Connecticut; Dr. Carl Pfeiffer of the Brain-Bio Center, Princeton, New Jersey; and Dr. Theron Randolph of Chicago, Illinois. In addition, I am also deeply indebted to CPC International for product information and help with recipes requiring special ingredients. Special thanks also go to the Bergen County, New Jersey, chapter of the Feingold Parents' Association and to the New York Institute For Child Development for sharing current information with me.

Every effort has been made to write a cookbook that would be of valuable help to you. Cooking for the hyperactive child is a complicated problem that can be surmounted if the whole family pulls together. My deepest wish is that this book will give you some new insights in coping with the special needs of your child.

Sincerely,

June Roth

Cooking for Your Hyperactive Child

1

Help for the Hyperactive Child

Thanks to the diligence of a few persevering doctors, parents and teachers have been made aware that the disruptive "brat" in the classroom may not be "just plain ornery" but may be suffering from a condition known as hyperkinesis. In more familiar terms, that child has a learning disability associated with hyperactivity.

But tagging a child with a term is not enough. We must be able to help that child to overcome the obnoxious behavior patterns that are disturbing the entire classroom. Today doctors, parents, and teachers are joining forces to get at the root of the problem and to find out why a particular child has uncontrollable bursts of energy, seems to be always in motion, and has unusually short spans of interest. Not the happy, bouncy, bubbling energy of most active youngsters, but rather the frantic chasing, racing, and chaotic behavior of a miserable little person who manages to turn teachers and peer groups into a hostile defensive reaction. On the home front, parents and siblings fare little better, although many times they seem to adapt and live with the "little terror" as best they can. It's not pleasant and there's a good chance that it may not even be necessary.

Some of these children have been helped to control their behavior problems by the use of a drug that is generically called "methyphenidate hydrocholoride." This often calms the effect but apparently does nothing to cure the cause. You can't just pop a pill into a hyperactive child's mouth and then pray it will prevent the kind of disruptive behavior in school that interferes with proper learning. There are new medical thoughts that indicate a need for other preventative measures to be taken right in your own kitchen. Or better yet, at the food market when you are choosing your family's provisions. It could make a difference.

Why involve the whole family when only one member is troubled? Because it will make it a healthier cuisine for all in the long view, and a healthier climate for the hyperactive child every day. And it's the one sure way you can prevent the wrong food from getting into the mouth of the afflicted child.

Doctors who are actively practicing preventative medicine claim that our modernized food, full of artificial additives, does not provide the right nutritional environment for hyperactive youngsters. You can turn the clock back in your own kitchen to create an old-fashioned natural food pantry that is free of artificial food coloring, artificial flavoring, and other additives.

It's not going to be easy. It may require relearning some cooking techniques, structuring your marketing selections differently, and facing the truth that you're going to be missing some products around the home that you have been using to make your meal preparation chores faster and easier. It's a small price to pay when the results may help the hyperactive child in your family to feel and behave calmer, and possibly help to overcome those feelings of frustration that accompany hyperactive behavior. Whether medication will still be indicated is up to your doctor, but the ultimate responsibility of feeding your child is in your own capable hands. If you've been wringing those hands and praying that there be some way that you could help this child, current thinking says that you can.

And that's not all you can do about this problem. Many specialists in this country and around the world state that food allergies often are the cause of some of the hyperactive child's problems. Not the kind of food allergies that cause one to break out in a rash, but rather the kind that causes either frenetic activity or withdrawn and depressed feelings. Some doctors say bosh and nonsense to these observations, but others have blazed medical trails to detect this sensitivity and then to help you to eliminate the offenders completely from the affected child's diet. Mostly it centers around the common foods we take for granted as part of our diet—dairy products, eggs, wheat, and corn. Sometimes it is a sensitivity to meat, fish, poultry, or a particular fruit or vegetable.

Regular scratch tests that are commonly used for allergy detection are not accurate enough in the area of neuro-allergy. But there are several ways to find out what the culprit food may be, if your child may be suffering in this way from a food sensitivity. Provocative intra-dermal and sub-lingual tests that some allergists now use can detect this type of allergy. Substances are injected under the skin or placed under the tongue to see whether there is a reaction. Positive reactions show up within fifteen minutes with these two tests.

Your doctor may prefer to test by using an "elimination diet." By this method, you take out one or more suspected food at a time from the child's diet for four full days each. Be sure to eliminate all forms of that particular food (lists of related foods appear in chapter 4) during the four days. On the fifth day, serve the child the eliminated food as lunch only. If there are no symptoms or ill-feelings after an hour, serve half the amount of the same food again, and a half hour later serve it again. If nothing happens within 12 hours, you can rule out that food as a likely cause of symptoms. Repeat this test, one food at a time, with all the major food groups, starting with the food that the child seems to eat more of than anything else. Does he crave huge quantities of milk? Start by eliminating that and all related products. It's best to keep a written record of everything eaten and all reactions.

Your doctor may prefer to oversee this food elimination diet in the hospital so that careful control may be taken to see that there is no access to other foods during the testing. Whichever way you do it, once you have found the food culprit you will have to remove it from the child's diet for an unknown period of time. (You will find more details about how to do this in a following chapter.) There is a chance that it can never be eaten again without disturbing reactions, or that it can be eaten only occasionally in a small quantity. The allergist should be able to give you good dietary guidance.

When you eliminate the food that causes reactions, plan your menus so that the child is always on a "rotary diet"—no food to be eaten more than once in four days. In addition, when planning such a four-day menu, be sure that no food of a related family is eaten more than once every two days. For instance, if you serve broccoli the first day, do not serve cabbage on the following day as it is a member of the same basic family of foods. You may however serve it on the third day of the four-day rotary diet, but you would then not serve Brussels sprouts on the fourth day—again because it is a member of the same basic family of foods, although it is a different vegetable on your menu. Allergists claim that this procedure will prevent a new food sensitivity from forming, which can happen with the too frequent ingestion of any one food or family of foods.

Occasionally a child is suffering from a problem related to an inadequate level of blood sugar and must have a severe limitation of sugar and other carbohydrates in the diet. A glucose-tolerance medical test might show whether there is such a problem of hypoglycemia, commonly known as low blood sugar, which requires a steadfast low-carbohydrate diet. Many doctors who are pioneering in the field of helping hyperactive children prefer that white and brown sugar be limited anyway, and that honey be used sparingly in its place. Be sure to discuss these factors with your doctor before formulating your own plan of attack on the problem from your kitchen.

In addition to eliminating all artificial additives from your food supply, having the child tested for possible food sensitivities and for possible hypoglycemia, some doctors believe that all foods containing natural salicylates (you'll find a list of these foods in Chapter 3) should be removed from the child's diet for a few weeks. Then they may be returned, one at a time every four days, unless there is a change in the child's behavior following any one of them. If so, eliminate it from the diet for a while and retest it at a later date to be sure. It is entirely possible that your doctor may decide to eliminate all natural salicylate foods for a longer period of time, while trying to map out a workable diet that will provide good solid nutrition for the child, and yet eliminate anything that may incite the kind of behavior that is spoiling your child's chance at a happier life.

Once you have the restrictions worked out, this book will help you to cook delicious meals for the whole family. The recipes have been chosen with the hyperactive child in mind, but in truth you are about to become a very good natural foods cook.

2

How to Eliminate Food Additives

If you can read you can eliminate artificial color, artificial flavorings, and preservatives from your market basket. It's all on the label of each article you pick up from the grocery shelves. At first it will be time consuming to read everything, so plan to spend a few hours at a time when you know the store to be uncrowded. Be sure to take a notebook along to jot down a list of "all right" brands whether you plan to purchase them that day or not. Then take your notebook along and save time on following marketing days, or write a planned shopping list and refer to your notebook at home.

What you are looking for are fresh foods that have not been enhanced with extra added color appeal or preservatives to add longer shelf life; frozen foods that have been flash frozen in their natural state, without added sauces and gravies; canned foods that may have salt added but nothing else; packaged foods that contain natural cereals, pasta made from natural ingredients, or natural ingredient breads.

It will help to be able to recognize all the chemical names to avoid, but there are actually many hundreds of them. Here is a list of some of the most frequently used additives in food at this time:

Artificial colors
Artificial flavorings

Butylated hydroxyanisole (BHA)
Butylated hydroxytoluene (BHT)
Brominated vegetable oil
Calcium propionate
Disodium benzoate
Gum arabic
Heptyl paraben
Monosodium glutamate (MSG)
Propylene glycol alginate
Saccharin
Sodium acid pyrophosphate
Sodium benzoate
Sodium nitrite
Sodium propionate

Once you have learned the names on the list above, it will help you to detect the chemical names of all the others. Armed with this information, let's start with the dairy products aisle of your food market.

Milk in all forms is a natural product. Avoid chocolate milk as it may not be made with pure chocolate. (Most allergists seem to cringe at the mere mention of chocolate anyway.) Read labels on dried milk—most well known brands are additive-free. If you are using butter for the whole family, you might want to consider using skim milk to cut down on the total butterfat content you are offering.

Sweet unsalted *butter* without added color is what you need for the hyperactive child. Most margarine has artificial coloring, so do not use it for the patient. If another member of the family must be on a low cholesterol diet, be sure to keep the margarine on a separate shelf in the refrigerator and alert all members of the family that it is not to be served to this child.

Yogurt is available in plain and natural flavors but check labels carefully to be sure there are no artificial colors or flavorings. Do not serve if child shows a sensitivity to yeast.

Sour cream is mostly natural but check labels.

Cottage cheese and *ricotta cheese* should have labels checked to find a natural brand.

Limit all *cheese* to natural varieties and most white cheeses; avoid colored processed American cheese—even the white variety usually has artificial color added. Avoid cheese spreads unless you have checked the labels.

Ice cream is available in natural flavors but you have to check brand labels carefully to find the few that do not contain artificial additives.

Eggs are fine in their natural form, but do not use egg substitutes or most frozen omelets, waffles, pancakes, or French toast unless you have checked the labels.

Usually the frozen foods counter is located near the dairy case, so that is the next logical area to do your food additive sleuthing. Avoid all prepared *frozen dinners* unless the label convinces you otherwise. The same goes for all *vegetables in sauce, sweetened fruits, frozen muffins, cakes,* and *juices.* If the label doesn't convince you that it is a pure product, don't buy it. Do buy all plain vegetables, unsweetened fruits such as strawberries (be sure there is no sugar added), pure fruit juices, and frozen fish that is additive-free.

Walk down the canned goods aisles for a look at the limited items available to you there. *Canned tuna* and other canned fish are all right if the label checks out pure. *Soups* are loaded with MSG and should be avoided. Plain canned vegetables and fruits (unsweetened) are all right most of the time, but watch out for special combinations that might have additives added. *Canned juices* that are pure may be used for drinking and even frozen into popsicles for snack-time treats. Check labels carefully to find some pure *spaghetti sauces.*

You'll be luckier as you take notes on the packaged items that may be used. Many are pure, but you must check the labels carefully to be sure. Most *old-fashioned cereals* such as cream of rice, cream of wheat, oatmeal, farina, grits, shredded wheat, puffed wheat, and puffed rice will be all right. Some corn flakes, raisin bran, and others may check out too.

Packaged pastas are often free of additives, as are *cornstarch, baking soda, baking powder, unflavored gelatin, white tapioca pearls, unbleached flour,* some cake mixes, some pancake mixes, and some pie-crust mixes. You'll find that most *cake mixes* are taboo, as well as most *gelatin* mixes, *pudding* mixes, *packaged dinners,* some *cocoa mixtures,* and most *cookies* and *crackers.* Some cookies and crackers will be all right, and many Scandinavian flat breads are pure too.

Look carefully at the *bottled items* such as *syrups, sauces,* and *condiments.* Choose light corn syrup and pure maple syrup for permitted breakfast use. Be sure that all *oils* are of a pure variety such as pure peanut oil, olive oil, soybean oil, corn oil, or other vegetable oil. Worcestershire sauce, pure soy sauce, Tabasco, most catsups, some mustards, and white vinegar are all right. Read labels of *salad dressings* with great care. Purchase *peanut butter* from a health food store or make it at home, if your doctor has advised against varieties that have sugar added—otherwise, look for a brand without additives. Check labels on *jams and jellies* to be sure that they are pure, if permission has been granted to use them occasionally.

Make your own *popcorn* from the pure packaged variety, check labels on *pretzels* and *potato chips*, which are usually all right; double check all *candy* labels to be sure that pure flavorings are included. *Nuts* and *dried fruits* are very good if the child has not been placed on a natural salicylate-free diet (more about this in Chapter 3). Pure carob that you can purchase in a health food store can often be substituted for chocolate, and pure peanut butter can be used for baking and candy making.

Fresh vegetables, fruit, fish, poultry and meat are always good, except for those vegetables and fruits listed on the natural salicylate-free diet, if it applies to your child. Do not use frankfurters, most sausages, bacon, and most packaged luncheon meats.

Buy only pure ingredient *breads*, rolls, and muffins, or learn to bake your own. The same goes for all cakes, cookies, and crackers.

It's a good idea to have snacks prepared for the hyperactive child, and to try to convince the rest of the family that it is unfair to bring any food into the house that will be appealing and harmful to the child. It just makes it harder to keep a diet going smoothly when enticing items are being eaten by others. You can help matters by keeping freshly scraped carrot and celery sticks in the refrigerator and plenty of fresh fruit. Apples and oranges should be fine, unless there has been a prescription for a natural salicylate-free diet.

If you can involve the child in baking cookies with you once a week, explaining the pure ingredients as you assemble them for mixing, you will be able to accomplish two things at once: You'll have a good time together; and you'll be teaching a lesson about the proper approach to food ingredients.

If the child can read, it's important to teach him to read food labels. The entire project of changing the household's food approach to fit the needs of the hyperactive child should include a "family meeting" where the goals are explained to all. You'll need all the cooperation you can get to keep the hyperactive child on a sensible diet, and the sensible eating patterns will benefit the entire family if you can make it a team effort.

3

What Foods Are Natural Salicylates

If the word salicylate seems familiar to you, it's probably because you have heard it before in connection with the common aspirin. Aspirin is a salicylate. So are a small number of foods—mostly fruits. Some doctors believe now that the hyperactive child should be taken off all natural salicylate foods while starting on a diet free of artificial colors and additives. If that is your doctor's prescription, here are the foods to eliminate:

Almonds
Apples (including cider and cider vinegar)
Apricots
Berries (blackberries, boysenberries, gooseberries, raspberries, and
    strawberries)
Cherries
Cloves
Cucumbers (including pickles)
Currants
Grapes (including dried raisins, wine, wine vinegar)
Mint
Nectarines

Oranges (other citrus fruits are all right)
Peaches
Plums (including prunes)
Tomatoes
Wintergreen

When the doctor gives permission to try to reinstate some of the natural salicylate foods, follow the directions in chapter 1, trying one food at a time no more than once every four days. If a reaction occurs, eliminate the food for the time being and try it again at a later date. If the same reaction occurs, take that food off your permissible list.

Make a list of these natural salicylate foods and tape it to the refrigerator door or tack it onto a kitchen pegboard. If it's out in the open for easy reference, there'll be less likelihood of mistakenly giving it to the child at the wrong time. Here again, if you explain it to the whole family at one sitting, you're more apt to have good results.

It's important to remember the "base foods" so that all subsidiary foods will be eliminated as well. An example of this is the forbidden use of grapes on this list. Grapes include all wines made with grapes, wine vinegar, and dried raisins. That means you'll have to exclude from the diet all breads, cakes, and cookies that have raisins. You will also need to read the labels on mustard and salad dressing bottles to determine which kind of vinegar has been used to make the mustard you are using (white vinegar is all right).

Probably the most difficult food to eliminate is tomatoes. It is used in catsup, sauces, soups, and stews. You'll have to alert the child and the rest of the family to the many uses of the tomato or they may still dump some catsup on his plate.

Naturally, this extra elimination complicates your food shopping list, but it is thought to be an important start to getting the hyperactive child on a carefully regulated diet. With a little luck, yours may be the child who can eat these foods again soon. Please rely on your allergist to guide you as to whether to exclude these foods. When permission is given to include them back into the child's menu, add them one at a time every four days and observe whether there is any behavioral reaction.

4

Related Allergy Foods and Menu Planning

If your child has been tested and deemed to have a sensitivity to any food, it's important to remember to eliminate also all the relatives to that food. When it is as simple as beets, you would only have to check the source of sugar to be sure that you are not serving beet sugar at any time, as well as eliminating the use of beets in all other forms completely. But if it is something like dairy products, eggs, wheat, or corn, your list will be considerably more complicated. The following should be of some help to you:

Sensitivity to Dairy Products

Eliminate all milk, buttermilk, chocolate milk, skim milk, cream, sour cream, yogurt, ice cream, and all products listing any of these as an ingredient. Watch out for nondairy products that may have milk protein solids in the base. Avoid all bakery products, cocoa mixes, creamed soups, creamed sauces, and all cheeses with the exception of those made from goat's milk. Bake with pure white vegetable shortening. Serve pure fruit ices, but don't use sherbets—they have milk as an ingredient. If the child is not sensitive to goat's milk, you may use that as a substitute drink—it is available in powdered form at your health foods store. You'll also find a dried soy milk powder there, but the taste cannot

11

compare to cow's milk. The child may prefer an allowable fruit juice with club soda for a bubbly beverage.

When dining in a restaurant, caution the child against ordering any creamed dishes, buttered vegetables, bread, cake, pies, puddings, junkets, omelets, rarebits, pancakes, or waffles. It is highly likely that they have been prepared with milk or butter. If in doubt, ask whether any type of milk or milk product, butter, margarine, cheese, or yogurt was used in the preparation of the food.

Sensitivity to Eggs

Eliminate eggs completely. Watch out for eggs used in baked goods, mayonnaise, salad dressings, sauces, griddle cakes, waffles, meat loaf, meatballs, malted cocoa drinks, pancake mixes, cake mixes, breads, and breaded foods. It is also used in ice creams, ices, pasta, and marshmallows. Do not permit the child to drink wine, as many wines are cleared with egg white. Read labels to be sure that dried egg is not listed as an ingredient of anything that will be served to the child.

Sensitivity to Wheat

Eliminate the use of wheat flour completely. Watch out for wheat and bran cereals, thick gravies, pancakes, waffles, breads, cookies, crackers, cakes, breaded foods, pasta, and even some candies. Don't rely on rye bread being made completely from rye flour; read the label as it is usually a combination of flour that includes wheat flour. Many people who have sensitivities to wheat have sensitivities to barley, rye, and oatmeal gluten too, so be sure to ascertain whether this is true in your child's case. If you are buying your flour at a health food store, read labels to be sure that the rye, rice, or corn flour is completely wheat-free. Don't order fried foods outside of the home because they may be dipped in flour first, or in a batter that has wheat in it, and the frying oil may even be contaminated through the use of wheat-coated products. This is probably the most difficult of sensitivities to deal with, and requires a lot of extra effort to track down permissible foods or to bake your own.

Sensitivity to Corn

Eliminate the use of corn completely. Watch out for cornstarch, corn meal, popcorn, corn oil, corn syrup, dextrose (glucose), hominy, grits, and corn bread. Cornstarch is a thickener that is found in many foods: in catsup, Chinese dishes, cough syrups, grape juice, ginger ale, ice cream, pasta, creamed pies, and cakes. Think of such surprise places as the adhesives used on stamps and envelopes, the composition of paper cups and plates, talcum powder, vitamin pills, and what have you. You'll have to be particularly vigilant to eliminate contact with corn, as subsidiary products are in use in many of the items we use every day.

To make recipe selection a little easier, all recipes in this book are marked so that you can easily eliminate any that contain a food your child is sensitive to. Notes are also made to alert you to a natural salicylate ingredient in case your doctor has prescribed avoiding them. Every effort has been made to develop recipes that children like and that the rest of the family will enjoy too.

Don't overlook the possibility of freezing certain special foods you have cooked to be served only to the child. There will be times when you are away from home, and these will come in handy. Look into the kitchen plastic bag sealers that come equipped with boilable bags. Just fill with the prepared food, heat seal, freeze, and then pop into boiling water to heat without diluting. It's the easy way to handle special diets in any house.

If the child is on a wheat-free regime that requires special purchases and special baking, you may want to keep those items separate in tightly closed containers. If the items are time-consuming to prepare or expensive, you may want to restrict their use to just the child involved.

When there are no food sensitivities after careful medical testing, it would be wise to plan your menus to eliminate artificial colors and artificial flavors for the hyperactive child, and to rotate foods so that no food allergy will develop. The best way to plan the meals is to be sure that the child has small portions of a variety of foods. Here's a review of basic nutrition facts for regular family menu planning:

Basic Nutrition Facts for Family Menu Planning

There are four groups of foods that must be included every day to attain good nutrition. They are:

The Meat Group
The Milk Group
The Vegetable–Fruit Group
The Bread–Cereal Group

Select your daily food servings in the following way:

The Meat Group

Eat two or more servings a day of meat, poultry, fish, eggs, dry beans, dry peas, lentils, or peanut butter. Each of the following is considered to be one serving:

2 to 3 ounces of boneless meat, poultry, or fish
2 eggs
1 cup cooked dry beans, dry peas, or lentils
4 tablespoons peanut butter

The Milk Group

Take in two or more 8-ounce servings of milk a day. Part or all of the milk may be skim milk, buttermilk, evaporated milk, or dry milk. Substitutions for milk may be made as follows:

1-inch wedge cheddar cheese equals ½ cup milk or 4 ounces
·½ cup cottage cheese equals ⅓ cup milk or 3 ounces
2 tablespoons cream cheese equals 1 tablespoon milk
½ cup ice cream equals ¼ cup milk or 2 ounces

If child is sensitive to dairy products your doctor probably will prescribe other methods of acquiring milk nutrients.

The Vegetable–Fruit Group

Eat four or more servings a day of a variety of fruits and vegetables.

Choose one serving of fruit or vegetable from the Vitamin A list at least every other day. Notice that these foods are all dark green or dark yellow in color; this will help you to remember them.

Choose one serving of citrus fruit or juice from the Vitamin C list every day, and one serving of vegetables from the Vitamin C list every day.

Choose the remaining servings from your own choice of fruits and vegetables or extra servings from the lists that follow.

Vitamin A Fruits: apricots, cantaloupe, mango, persimmon
Vitamin A Vegetables: broccoli, carrots, chard, collards, cress, kale, pumpkin, spinach, sweet potatoes, turnip greens, winter squash

Vitamin C Fruits: grapefruit, guava, honeydew melon, lemon, mango, orange, papaya, strawberries, tangerine, watermelon

Vitamin C Vegetables: asparagus, broccoli, Brussels sprouts, cabbage, collards, cress, green pepper, kale, kohlrabi, mustard greens, potatoes and sweet potatoes cooked in jackets, spinach, sweet red peppers, tomatoes, turnip greens.

The Bread–Cereal Group

Eat four or more servings a day. Each of the following is considered to be one serving:

1 slice bread
1 ounce ready-to-eat cereal
½ cup cooked cereal, cornmeal, grits, macaroni, noodles, rice, or spaghetti

This is the way your "daily dozen" adds up:

2 servings of Meat Group
2 servings of Milk Group
4 servings of Vegetable-Fruit Group
4 servings of Bread-Cereal Group
= Daily Dozen for Good Health

Additional food energy and other food values can be obtained from foods that are not in these four food groups. These include all varieties of fats and sweets. Extra servings of the four food groups will be helpful to maintain good nutrition.

This information should make it easier for you to plan your menus. Following is a sample four-day menu plan that provides good balanced nutrition and is free of natural salicylates. It is intended for the child who has no proven allergy to any food, but who has been advised to follow a salicylate-free/additive-free diet. Unaffected family members may add the eliminated natural salicylate foods as desired. This is not a rotary diet. (If you have been advised to place the child on a four-day *rotary diet*, where you do not repeat a serving of *any* food item within that time, follow the Four-Day Diversified Rotary Diet instead.)

Special diets are usually more difficult to prepare and to continue to supervise. It takes a lot of willingness and effort on your part to bring about family cooperation and proper food management for the child. If you find that the behavior of the child improves it will all be worth it.

There are many case histories to show that others have tried these methods with success. Here's hoping that it will help your child too.

**Four-Day Good Nutrition Natural Salicylate-Free Diet
(unaffected family members may add removed foods as desired)**

FIRST DAY:

Breakfast
Glass grapefruit juice
1 egg, any style
Rye toast and butter
Milk or allowable beverage

Lunch
Tuna salad and lettuce sandwich
Carrot sticks
Banana
Milk or allowable beverage

Dinner
Pea soup
Lamb chops
Baked potato
Broccoli
Biscuit and butter
Oatmeal cookie
Milk or allowable beverage

SECOND DAY:

Breakfast
Glass pineapple juice
Shredded wheat
Milk or allowable beverage

Lunch
Hamburger on bun with pure catsup and onion
Coleslaw
Watermelon slice
Milk or allowable beverage

Dinner
Mushroom–barley soup
Broiled chicken
Rice
Green beans
Corn muffin and butter
Fresh or canned pear
Milk or allowable beverage

THIRD DAY:

Breakfast
Glass cranberry juice
Cooked farina
Milk or allowable beverage

Lunch
Grilled natural cheese sandwich
Crisp peanut butter cookie
Milk or allowable beverage

Dinner
Wedge of melon
Veal pot roast
Baked sweet potato
Cooked spinach with butter
Vanilla pudding
Milk or allowable beverage

FOURTH DAY:

Breakfast
Fresh blueberries
Buckwheat pancakes with butter
Milk or allowable beverage

Lunch
Sliced turkey sandwich
Crisp celery sticks
Chocolate–peanut butter brownie
Milk or allowable beverage

Dinner
½ grapefruit
Fillet of sole
Baked macaroni and cheese
Zucchini
Bran muffin and butter
Sour cream coffee cake
Milk or allowable beverage

To Help You to Understand
the Four-Day Diversified Rotary Diet

This is the most difficult eating pattern to try to achieve. What it means is that your child will not eat the same food more than once in four days, and no related food more than once in two days.

Grains, such as wheat, barley, rye, oats, corn, and rice should be assigned to one meal in the four days. If you have used the grain in one meal, don't use it in any other form in another meal within the four-day spread. Do not use the gluten-related grains of wheat, barley, rye, and oats more than once every two days. If you splurge and have wheat pancakes made with eggs and milk, you may as well have butter on them and drink a glass of milk with them too. Then cross wheat, eggs, and milk off your list for four days—the party with those items is over. Two days later you may have barley *or* rye *or* oats at one meal.

When using milk or a milk product once, you have a choice of using it as a beverage, a cheese, yogurt, or even a combination of several at the same meal. But that is the only time to use it during the four days.

You may find fruits and vegetables on this suggested menu that the child has never eaten before. It's time to expand those taste buds to take advantage of every different kind of food available. Keep in mind that there are certain "families" of foods that should not be repeated more than once every two days. Let's talk about the legume family—it includes peas, beans, lima beans, chick peas, and so on. If you serve the child peas once in the four-day period, try not to serve a legume the next day. You may serve another one of the legumes on day three. The same goes for the cabbage family—that includes broccoli, Brussels sprouts, cauliflower, red cabbage, and white cabbage. Serve your choice one day and serve none of them the next day. Remember that all forms of squash and melons are related, apples and pears are related, and the citrus family of oranges, grapefruit, lemons, and limes are related too. Take careful notice of how these food families have been rotated through the four-day menu plan.

Where orange juice is indicated, remember that an orange may be eaten in its place. Certain fish dishes are suggested, but you may vary your menu with others. If the child has eaten a beef meal in the four days, do not include a veal meal—they are actually the same animal. You may change the menus around any way you wish, as long as the same food is not eaten twice in four days.

In this following set of menus, all natural salicylate foods have been starred so they may easily be removed if the patient has been placed on a natural salicylate-free diet.

Keep notes on after effects of any meal to discuss with your doctor. If something in that meal has caused a reaction, you will have a short list of foods to work with. That will enable the doctor to further hunt for another sensitivity that can be eliminated from the diet to promote well being.

Here are some other hints on how to get along on a Rotary Diet:

• Assign each kind of grain to a different meal. Then serve another preparation of the same grain at the same meal. An example would be to eat corn on the cob and a corn muffin made from corn meal. Another would be to have pasta and wheat bread at the same meal.

• Whenever you serve a certain kind of juice, eat a piece of that fruit for dessert at that meal. An example would be starting with apple juice and having applesauce for dessert. The same trick goes for vegetables too—consider having tomato juice at the same meal you have a sliced tomato.

• If the child is anxious for a piece of cake, save the wheat and eggs for that meal. Then he can enjoy an omelet and wheat toast too.

• Although beef and veal are related, pork, lamb, goat, chicken, duck, turkey, and every other kind of poultry and fish stand alone. That gives you a wide range of protein choices to play with.

• Don't overlook the variety available in cooking oils. You can rotate them as you do your meal ingredients. If something is going to be fried at a meal when you are eating corn, use corn oil for the frying. Vary with safflower oil, olive oil, peanut oil, and every other salad oil you can find.

• Try not to waste a lot of vegetables in one salad, unless you have planned the remaining four days very well. Instead, combine lettuce with just one vegetable, and make salads of cold sliced vegetables that lend themselves to this use. For example, combine fresh spinach leaves with sliced fresh mushrooms; or slice cucumber paper thin and marinate in vinegar and water; or serve cooked cold sliced beets that have been chilled with thin slivers of onion.

• Write your menus down. It's the only way to keep track of what has been eaten at a particular meal. It's also a good way to get a look at what may be added safely to make this four-day diet a treat instead of a treatment.

Four-Day Diversified Rotary Diet

FIRST DAY:

Breakfast
*Sliced orange or orange juice
Rye flatbread (no wheat)
Peanut butter

Lunch
Fillet of sole, flounder, or cod fish
Carrots
Celery
Sliced pineapple

Dinner
Cooked artichoke or canned artichoke hearts
Broiled lamb chop or sliced lamb roast
Acorn squash, hubbard squash, or mashed cooked pumpkin
Spinach
*Apricots

NOTE: A portion of melon may be substituted for squash or pumpkin, and eaten any time during this day.

SECOND DAY:

Breakfast
Blueberries
2 eggs boiled, poached, or scrambled in safflower oil

Lunch
Canned salmon or tuna, packed in water
Lettuce
Broiled or sliced tomato
Banana

Dinner
Broiled chicken or roast duck
Baked potato
Broccoli, Brussels sprouts, or cauliflower
Pear halves

THIRD DAY:

Breakfast
½ grapefruit
Cottage cheese, yogurt, or other cheese or milk product

Lunch
Shrimp, clams, lobster, mussels, scallops, or haddock
Rice
Peas, green beans, lima beans, or chick peas
*Sliced peaches, plums, or nectarines

Dinner
Beef or veal patties, or cooked sliced beef or veal
Onions
Mushrooms
Zucchini or crookneck yellow squash
Corn
*Strawberries

NOTE: Onions and mushrooms may be sautéed in a small amount of corn oil.

FOURTH DAY:

Breakfast
Cranberry juice
Oatmeal cereal (no milk), or pure wheat cereal (no milk), or wheat
　　toast

Lunch
Sliced turkey with natural gravy
Asparagus
Beets
Kadota figs

Dinner
Pork chops, pork roast, baked bass or red snapper
Baked sweet potato
Cooked red or white cabbage
 *Baked apple or applesauce

NOTE: Broccoli, Brussels sprouts, or cauliflower may be substituted for cooked cabbage, but do not eat same food again for four days.

---

* Contains natural salicylates. Omit if necessary.

5

Appetizers

Does it seem that the hours between school and dinner stretch out into one long "hungry hour" at your house? Somehow the best of menu planning seems to get disrupted by a child's need to nibble before supper. What's the best way to cope?

Have a selection of nutritious drinks handy that will be appealing to all the children and not interfere with the special diet program for the hyperactive child. Offer plain milk, plain fruit juice or add club soda for a bubbly effect, or fresh vegetable juice made with an electric juice extractor. Whenever you permit the child to have soda pop, be sure that is is a noncola, colorless, sugarless variety.

Scraped fresh vegetables will provide immediate crunch and nutrition at the same time. A dip will make it more appealing for everyone.

If a big bowl of snacks is in order, try freshly popped corn with real melted butter (if there's no corn or dairy sensitivity), roasted soybeans, unsalted peanuts, or fresh fruit. You'll probably be able to find pretzels and potato chips without artificial additives, but check the kind of oil used for deep-frying the chips.

A bowl of crackers with a smaller bowl of nutritious cheese, tuna, or liver spread may be appreciated, and you can tag it as a first course for dinner.

Watch the child with a sweet tooth who begs for lollipops and colored candies—just don't have them around. Instead, serve cracker jack or pure peanut brittle. You can make your own candy from recipes in chapter 15 that will be less expensive and provide some togetherness fun too. Shop the health food stores for carob bars that have a similar taste to chocolate, halvah (unless your child is on a natural salicylate-free diet as it's made of ground almonds), or dried fruit.

You can prepare your own gelatin with unflavored gelatin and fruit juice—slice some bananas into it for an extra surprise. Make your own popsicles by freezing fruit juice in plastic forms, available with the necessary sticks at your local housewares department store.

If you expect the demand for snacks in the afternoon, you'll be prepared for the occasion. Most of the recipes in this chapter will do double duty as snacks and predinner cocktail appetizers. Don't serve the hyperactive child a "Shirley Temple" cocktail—the ginger ale will be all right, but the maraschino cherry has been treated to a red color bath.

Creamy Dip

SENSITIVITY CHECKLIST:

This recipe is

dairy _____-free

egg ✓_____-free

wheat ✓_____-free

corn ✓_____-free

sugar ✓_____-free

Serve this dip with an assortment of raw vegetables such as carrot sticks, celery sticks, pieces of cauliflower, zucchini strips and cherry tomatoes (if child is not on a natural salicylate-free diet).

1 cup dairy sour cream
1 teaspoon grated onion
1 teaspoon salt
½ teaspoon grated lemon rind
1½ tablespoons lemon juice
¼ teaspoon pure soy sauce

Beat sour cream until light and fluffy. Add the remaining ingredients and mix well. Chill.

Makes more than 1 cup of dip.

Cheese-stuffed Mushrooms

SENSITIVITY CHECKLIST:

This recipe is _____-free (dairy)

✓ -free (egg)

✓ -free (wheat)

✓ -free (corn)

✓ -free (sugar)

Mushrooms can be stuffed ahead of time and refrigerated. Slip under the broiler just before serving.

24 large fresh mushrooms
½ cup cottage cheese
½ teaspoon garlic salt
¼ teaspoon pure Worcestershire sauce
¼ teaspoon thyme
Paprika

Wash mushrooms; remove stems and chop finely. Combine chopped stems, cottage cheese, garlic salt, Worcestershire sauce and thyme; spoon into mushroom caps. Sprinkle with paprika. Place stuffed mushroom caps in a small broiling pan and broil for 5 minutes or until cheese is lightly browned.

Makes 2 dozen appetizers.

Broiled Cheese Puffs

SENSITIVITY CHECKLIST:

This recipe is    ____-free **dairy**

____-free **egg**

____-free **wheat**

✓ -free **corn**

✓ -free **sugar**

Prepare the cheese mixture in advance. Cover and refrigerate until you are ready to broil the puffs.

1 cup finely grated Swiss cheese
2 tablespoons chopped ripe olives
1 tablespoon finely chopped green pepper
Dash of garlic salt
¼ cup mayonnaise (see Index)
18 Melba toast rounds
Paprika

Combine cheese, olives, green pepper, and garlic salt. Add mayonnaise and mix well. Spoon onto toast rounds. Sprinkle with paprika. Place in a broiling pan and slip under the broiler for about 3 minutes or until puffy and lightly browned. Serve hot.

Makes 18 puffs.

Date–Nut Spread

SENSITIVITY CHECKLIST:

This recipe is dairy _____-free

egg ✔ free

wheat ✔-free

corn ✔-free

sugar ✔-free

If child has been placed on a natural salicylate-free diet, omit raisins in this recipe.

1 cup cottage cheese
½ cup finely chopped dates
½ cup raisins
⅓ cup chopped pecans
½ teaspoon salt

Beat cottage cheese in a small bowl until fairly smooth. Stir in dates, raisins, pecans, and salt. Use as a spread or sandwich filling.

Makes about 1⅔ cups.

Liptauer Cheese

SENSITIVITY CHECKLIST:

This recipe is  _____-free

dairy

✓-free

egg

✓-free

wheat

✓-free

corn

✓-free

sugar

For the family occasions that involve children and a predinner nibbling hour, this cheese spread with crackers is safe and delicious. Check labels on anchovy and capers if child is sensitive to corn, to be sure that it is not listed in the packing oil.

2 tablespoons dried parsley flakes
1 cup butter, softened
1 package (8 ounces) cream cheese, softened
3 anchovy fillets, chopped
1 teaspoon dry mustard
1 teaspoon paprika
1 teaspoon finely chopped onion
1 teaspoon chopped capers
1 teaspoon chopped chives
1 teaspoon finely chopped parsley
½ teaspoon caraway seeds

Coat the inside of a 2-cup bowl with butter; sprinkle with parsley flakes to cover all sides. In separate bowl, stir soft butter into softened cream cheese until well mixed. Add anchovies, mustard, paprika, onion, capers, chives, parsley, and caraway seeds. Press mixture into coated bowl. Chill 4 hours or until firm. Unmold before serving.

Makes 2 cups.

Chopped Sardine Salad

SENSITIVITY CHECKLIST:

This recipe is   **dairy**   ✔ -free

   egg   _____ free

   wheat   ✔ -free

   corn   ✔ -free

   sugar   _____-free

Sardines are gaining in popularity again because they are high in nutrients. The boneless and skinless imported variety are a delicacy.

2 cans (3¾ ounces each) sardines, drained and broken in pieces
2 hard-cooked eggs, chopped
¼ cup chopped onion
2 tablespoons mayonnaise (see Index)
2 tablespoons plain yogurt
2 tablespoons white vinegar
1½ tablespoons sugar

Mix the sardines, egg, and onion together. Stir the mayonnaise, yogurt, vinegar, and sugar together; add this mixture to the sardine mixture and stir. Chill for several hours. Serve as an appetizer or sandwich filling.

Makes 1⅔ cups.

Tuna Cheese Spread

SENSITIVITY CHECKLIST:

This recipe is   〔〕   _____-free
           dairy

            ○   ✓-free
            egg

            ⸸   ✓-free
           wheat

            🌽   ✓-free
           corn

            🥣   ✓-free
           sugar

This spread is a good sandwich filling too. Especially good for those on an egg-free diet as it does not even require the addition of mayonnaise.

1 can (7 ounces) water-packed tuna, drained and flaked
¼ cup cottage cheese
¼ cup plain yogurt
2 tablespoons finely chopped onion
1 teaspoon white horseradish
¼ teaspoon pure Worcestershire sauce
Melba toast rounds or crackers

Mix the tuna and cottage cheese together. Add yogurt, onion, horseradish, and Worcestershire sauce. Mix well. Chill. Spread on crackers or place in a bowl for do-it-yourself spreading.

Makes 1½ cups or enough for 36 crackers.

Creamed Tuna–Cheese Spread

SENSITIVITY CHECKLIST:

This recipe is   _____-free
dairy

_____-free
egg

__✔__-free
wheat

__✔__-free
corn

__✔__-free
sugar

Read the labels carefully to make sure that the crackers you serve are free from artificial colors and flavorings.

1 can (7 ounces) tuna, drained and flaked
1 package (3 ounces) cream cheese
2 tablespoons mayonnaise (see Index)
2 tablespoons dairy sour cream
1 tablespoon grated onion
½ teaspoon prepared white horseradish
¼ teaspoon pure Worcestershire sauce

Mix tuna and cream cheese. Add the remaining ingredients and mix well. Chill. Place in a bowl for do-it-yourself spreading on crackers or toast rounds.

Makes 1½ cups of spread.

Chopped Chicken Livers

SENSITIVITY CHECKLIST:

This recipe is ___✓___-free

___-free

___✓___-free

___✓___-free

___✓___-free

No need to fry chicken livers in fat when you can use this simmering method to get a fine textured pâté. If child has been placed on an egg-free diet, increase the amount of onion and take child's portion off before adding eggs.

1 pound fresh chicken livers
1 onion, sliced thin
2 hard-cooked eggs
¼ teaspoon salt
⅛ teaspoon pepper

Place chicken livers and sliced onion rings in a large skillet; barely cover the bottom of the skillet with water. Cover and simmer for five minutes, turning the livers occasionally and adding more water if needed to keep livers from sticking to the pan. Chop or grind livers, onions, and hard-cooked eggs together; stir in just enough pan juices to hold the mixture together. Add salt and pepper; chill until ready to use. Serve as a spread with crackers, as a first course, or as a luncheon salad.

Makes about 1½ cups of chopped liver.

Chopped Eggplant

SENSITIVITY CHECKLIST:

This recipe is  ✓-free *dairy*

✓-free *egg*

✓-free *wheat*

✓-free *corn*

✓-free *sugar*

This is an inexpensive and tasty spread for crackers or stuffing for celery stalks. Nice to serve as an appetizer course too.

1 medium eggplant
1 small onion, diced
2 tablespoons lemon juice
¾ teaspoon salt
¼ teaspoon pepper
½ teaspoon oregano
1 tablespoon peanut oil

Bake the whole eggplant, uncovered, in a 350° F. oven until the skin turns dark brown and is wrinkled. Remove from oven, cut the skin away, and then cut eggplant into several thick manageable slices. Place these in a large chopping bowl, add the onion, and chop together until it is all very fine. Add lemon juice, salt, pepper, and oregano; stir well. Then add peanut oil and stir again. Chill.

Makes about 2 cups.

Shrimp Balls

SENSITIVITY CHECKLIST:

This recipe is   dairy   _____-free

egg   ✓-free

wheat   ✓-free

corn   ✓-free

sugar   ✓-free

This is special occasion or party food that makes a tasty bite. And the bonus is that they can be prepared ahead.

½ pound shrimp, cooked and cleaned
1 package (3 ounces) cream cheese
¼ cup finely diced celery
2 teaspoons grated onion
1 teaspoon white horseradish
1 teaspoon pure Worcestershire sauce
¼ teaspoon salt
¼ cup finely chopped fresh parsley

Chop shrimp very fine. Mash cream cheese until soft and fluffy; add chopped shrimp. Add celery, onion, horseradish, Worcestershire sauce, and salt. Form into ½-inch balls. Roll in chopped parsley. Chill.

Makes about 2 dozen balls.

Pizza Wedges

SENSITIVITY CHECKLIST:

This recipe is   ____-free
    dairy

     ✓ -free
    egg

     ____-free
    wheat

     ✓ -free
    corn

     ____-free
    sugar

If child is placed on a natural salicylate-free diet, omit this recipe until permission is granted to add tomatoes to the diet again. Muffins have milk, wheat, and sugar ingredients; check label for egg in the product if there is an egg sensitivity.

**1 cup pure tomato sauce
1 tablespoon olive oil
½ teaspoon oregano
4 English muffins, split
1 package (8 ounces) mozzarella cheese slices
3 tablespoons grated Parmesan cheese**

Combine tomato sauce, olive oil, and oregano. Arrange English muffin halves on an ungreased cookie sheet. Spoon tomato sauce mixture onto each muffin half; top with a slice of mozzarella cheese and sprinkle with Parmesan cheese. Broil for about 3 minutes or until cheese is melted and lightly browned. Cut each muffin half into quarters.

Makes 32 wedges; 4 to 8 servings.

6

Soup

This is the category of food that probably hits the modern cook hardest when coping with a hyperactive child's special diet. Canned and packaged dried soups are out. That puts a real cramp into the style of the reach-for-a-can-of-soup homemaker. You have a choice. Let the rest of the family have the convenience food soups with additives, or abolish them and learn how to cook soup from scratch.

Maybe you'll compromise and do both. Just be sure that no one slips and serves the child the wrong soup. Once you have mastered the art of homemade soup, you'll find it easier to give up the other kind altogether.

When you think of a soup pot, think big. Set a soup making day if you wish to each week—all you need to start are a chicken or some bones, or even just vegetables and water. You might start with one kind of soup and by adding leftovers to it during the week have a different kind of soup every day. It's healthy and it's economical too.

If you prefer to cook for the child alone, make the soup and freeze it for future use. By stockpiling several kinds of soup, you'll have a variety on hand at all times.

Another trick is to freeze chicken bouillon in ice cube trays. When you have some vegetable leftovers, place them in the electric blender with some thawed soup cubes and blend the child a smooth vegetable soup;

heat and serve. It's a fast workable trick for days when you're in a hurry.

Add cooked rice, noodles, macaroni, barley, or the very fine pastina for extra good taste and texture. And don't forget to add some toppings just for fun—a spoonful of popped corn, a dollop of sour cream, toasted croutons, unsalted peanuts, or even grated coconut. When you keep meals full of surprises and interesting tastes and textures, it's easier to rotate the diet and keep the menu from getting into a rut.

This chapter has many soups to start you on your way to making hearty soups, imaginative soups, use-up-the-leftovers soups, and even motherly chicken soup.

Tomato Soup

SENSITIVITY CHECKLIST:

This recipe is   dairy ___✓___-free

egg ___✓___-free

wheat ___✓___-free

corn ___✓___-free

sugar _____-free

If the child has been placed on a natural salicylate-free diet, omit this recipe until permission has been granted to resume the use of tomatoes. Sugar can be omitted from this recipe if desired.

2 meaty beef neck bones
1 can (28 ounces) tomatoes in natural juice
3 cups water
3 tablespoons rice
1 onion, diced
½ teaspoon salt
¼ teaspoon pepper
¼ teaspoon basil

Place neck bones in a heavy saucepan. Add tomatoes, water, rice, and onion. Stir. Add sugar, salt, pepper, and basil. Bring to a boil, reduce heat, cover, and simmer for 2 hours. Stir occasionally. Serve with bits of neck meat.

Makes 6 servings.

Cream of Tomato Soup

SENSITIVITY CHECKLIST:

This recipe is   _____-free *dairy*

✓-free *egg*

_____-free *wheat*

✓-free *corn*

✓-free *sugar*

If the child has been placed on a natural salicylate-free diet omit this recipe until permission has been granted to resume the use of tomatoes.

1 can (1 pound) tomatoes in natural juice
1 small onion, sliced
1 sprig parsley
1 bay leaf
1 teaspoon salt
¼ teaspoon cayenne
1 teaspoon pure Worcestershire sauce
4 cups water
3 tablespoons butter
3 tablespoons flour

Empty tomatoes into a saucepan. Add sliced onion, parsley, bay leaf, salt, cayenne, Worcestershire sauce, and water. Cook for 20 minutes. Press through a sieve or food mill. Melt butter in a small saucepan; add flour and stir until smooth. Pour some of the tomato soup into the butter–flour mixture, and stir until very smooth; then gradually return this mixture to the tomato soup, stirring constantly. Heat and stir for several minutes before serving.

Makes 6 servings.

Oyster Stew

This recipe is   *dairy* _____-free

egg _✓_-free

wheat _✓_-free

corn _✓_-free

sugar _✓_-free

This can be a traditional start to a Thanksgiving dinner or any other festive occasion. Or serve it as a main course with an ample salad on the side.

1 pint shucked oysters, with liquor
1 quart milk
¼ cup butter
1 sprig fresh dill
½ teaspoon salt
⅛ teaspoon pepper

In a 4-quart pan cook oysters, with liquor, over low heat until edges of oysters just begin to curl. Add milk, butter, dill, salt, and pepper. Heat slowly until hot; do not boil.

Makes about 6 servings.

Spinach Soup

SENSITIVITY CHECKLIST:

This recipe is ⬜ _____-free (dairy)

○ _✓_-free (egg)

_✓_-free (wheat)

_✓_-free (corn)

_✓_-free (sugar)

Add a little heavy cream to the Spinach Soup if you like a creamy soup. Either way, it's a good healthy start to any meal.

1 package (10 ounces) frozen chopped spinach
3 cups chicken broth (see Index)
1 hot boiled potato, peeled
2 tablespoons butter
½ teaspoon salt
⅛ teaspoon pepper
⅛ teaspoon nutmeg

Cook spinach as directed on the package; drain. Put in blender with 1 cup of the chicken broth and the boiled potato. Blend until smooth. Pour remaining chicken broth into a saucepan; add butter, salt, pepper, and nutmeg. Stir in blended spinach mixture. Heat and serve.

Makes 6 servings.

Split Pea Soup

SENSITIVITY CHECKLIST:

This recipe is ✓-free
dairy

✓-free
egg

✓-free
wheat

✓-free
corn

✓-free
sugar

This soup is well worth the time to cook and it keeps well in the refrigerator for several days. Particularly good on a cold winter day.

2 cups dried split peas
2 quarts water
2 meaty beef neck bones
2 onions, diced
2 carrots, scraped and finely diced
2 stalks celery, finely diced
Several sprigs of parsley, minced
Several sprigs of fresh dill, minced
¾ teaspoon salt
¼ teaspoon pepper

Place split peas in a heavy saucepan and add water. Add remaining ingredients and stir. Bring to a boil, then turn the heat low, cover and simmer for 2½ to 3 hours. Stir occasionally. To serve, remove bones and strain through a food mill if smooth soup is desired. Otherwise serve as it is with bits of meat from the bones.

Makes 8 servings.

Cream of Celery Soup

SENSITIVITY CHECKLIST:

This recipe is **dairy** _____-free

egg ✓-free

wheat _____-free

corn ✓-free

sugar ✓-free

Serve this as indicated one night, then deliberately cook extra vegetables and blend leftover soup and vegetables together into a new soup for the following night. It's just one way the electric blender can make your life easier and more interesting.

1 bunch celery, finely chopped
1 quart water
1 onion, finely diced
1 teaspoon salt
¼ teaspoon nutmeg
¼ teaspoon celery salt
¼ teaspoon cayenne
3 tablespoons butter
3 tablespoons flour
2 cups milk

Place celery in a deep saucepan; add water, onion, salt, nutmeg, celery salt, and cayenne. Bring to a boil, then reduce heat and simmer until celery and onion are soft and tender. Melt butter; stir in flour, and then milk. Cook for several minutes, stirring constantly. Stir this mixture into the celery mixture and simmer for 5 minutes, stirring until smooth.

Makes 8 to 10 servings.

Potato Soup

This recipe is

        ____-free (dairy)

        ✓-free (egg)

        ✓-free (wheat)

        ____-free (corn)

        ✓-free (sugar)

If child is sensitive to corn, substitute wheat flour for cornstarch in this recipe. If you prefer a smooth soup, press mixture through a sieve or use an electric blender.

3 large potatoes, diced
1 leek or small onion, finely diced
2 stalks celery, finely diced
½ teaspoon salt
⅛ teaspoon pepper
½ teaspoon dried dill
1 quart milk
2 tablespoons butter
2 tablespoons cornstarch

Put diced potato, leek or onion, celery, salt, pepper, and dill in a large saucepan; barely cover with water and cook until potatoes are soft. Add milk and butter; simmer and stir until butter is melted. Stir cornstarch with just enough enough water to make a smooth thin paste; spoon some of the hot soup liquid into this paste and then return the entire mixture to the soup, stirring constantly. Continue to stir and cook until soup thickens; do not boil.

Makes 8 servings.

Fish Chowder

SENSITIVITY CHECKLIST:

This recipe is

If child is sensitive to corn, substitute wheat flour for the cornstarch in the recipe below. This soup is hearty enough to be a main course. A green and yellow vegetable salad rounds out the nutrition.

1½ pounds fillet of haddock, flounder, or cod
1 large onion, diced
2 large potatoes, diced
2 stalks celery, finely diced
1 quart milk
2 tablespoons butter
½ teaspoon salt
¼ teaspoon pepper
¼ teaspoon thyme
2 tablespoons cornstarch

Place fish in a large saucepan; cover with water and cook until fish falls apart easily. Add onion, potatoes, and celery, and simmer until they are tender. Add milk, butter, salt, pepper, and thyme. Simmer and stir until butter is melted. Stir cornstarch with just enough water to make a smooth thin paste; spoon some of the hot soup liquid into this paste and then return the entire mixture to the soup, stirring constantly. Continue to stir and cook until soup thickens slightly. Then serve at once.

Makes 8 to 10 servings.

Onion Soup

SENSITIVITY CHECKLIST:

This recipe is   ____-free

✓ -free

____-free

✓ -free

____-free

Soup doesn't have to come from a can when you are able to cook it this fast and this good. Float a piece of toasted French bread in each bowl and pass extra Parmesan cheese.

2 cups onions, thinly sliced
3 tablespoons butter
¼ teaspoon brown sugar
1 teaspoon salt
¼ teaspoon pepper
2 tablespoons flour
4 cups water
2 tablespoons Parmesan cheese

Sauté onions in butter in the bottom of a saucepan. Sprinkle brown sugar over onions to aid in browning. Add salt and pepper. Add flour and cook, stirring constantly, until mixture is smooth and thick. Gradually stir in water, until smooth. Cook over low heat, covered, for 20 minutes. Stir in cheese just before serving.

Makes 4 servings.

Cream of Corn Soup

SENSITIVITY CHECKLIST:

This recipe is _____-free dairy

____✓__-free egg

____✓__-free wheat

_____-free corn

____✓__-free sugar

This is a quick soup that children love. Only those sensitive to corn or dairy products need to omit this soup. Be sure to read labels before buying canned corn, although most are prepared without additives.

1 can (12 ounces) whole kernel corn
1 can (1 pound) natural creamed corn (no artificial additives)
2 cups milk
1 tablespoon butter
½ teaspoon salt
⅛ teaspoon pepper

Combine the cans of corn and milk in a saucepan. Add butter, salt, and pepper. Heat thoroughly, stirring constantly, until butter is melted and blended.

Makes 6 servings.

Vegetable Soup

SENSITIVITY CHECKLIST:

This recipe is  ___✓___-free

___✓___-free

___✓___-free

___✓___-free

___✓___-free

If the child has been placed on a natural salicylate-free diet, omit to-matoes until permission has been given to resume their use. Cut shreds of beef from the bones to add to the soup and don't hesitate to add other vegetables you may have available. Avoid those in the cabbage family as they tend to dominate the flavor of the soup.

2 pounds of beef neck bones
2 quarts water
2 onions, diced
2 carrots, scraped and diced
2 stalks celery, diced
1 teaspoon salt
¼ teaspoon pepper
1 pound lima beans, soaked for several hours
1 potato, peeled and diced
1 can (1 pound) tomatoes in natural juice
1 package (10 ounces) frozen cut green beans
1 package (10 ounces) frozen peas

Place bones and water in a deep pot. Bring to a boil, then simmer for 30 minutes. Skim residue from the top with a spoon. Add onions, carrots, celery, salt, and pepper. Simmer, covered, for 1 hour. Add soaked lima beans and simmer for 30 minutes. Add potato, tomatoes, green beans, and peas. Simmer 30 minutes more. Taste and add additional salt and pepper if needed.

Makes 8 servings.

Mushroom–Barley Soup

SENSITIVITY CHECKLIST:

This recipe is

        dairy   ✓ -free

        egg   ✓ -free

        wheat   ✓ -free

        corn   ✓ -free

        sugar   ✓ -free

Here's a hearty soup that freezes well. For individual servings in a hurry, pack in boilable bags and heat seal. Be sure to mark the bag with a waterproof pen as everything begins to look alike when it is frozen.

1 pound short ribs of beef, or several meaty bones
2 quarts water
1 cup barley
1 onion, diced
2 carrots, scraped and diced
2 stalks celery, finely diced
½ pound fresh mushrooms, sliced
1 teaspoon salt
¼ teaspoon pepper
2 sprigs fresh dill

Place beef (or bones) and water in a deep pot. Add barley. Simmer over low heat for 1 hour. Skim surface with a large spoon. Add rest of ingredients and simmer, stirring occasionally, for 1 hour more.

Makes 8 servings.

NOTE: Meat may be served separately, or trimmed of fat and cut up into the soup.

Chicken Soup

SENSITIVITY CHECKLIST:

This recipe is   **dairy**   ✓ -free

   egg   ✓ -free

   wheat   ✓ -free

   corn   ✓ -free

   sugar   ✓ -free

Freeze extra broth in an ice cube tray. When frozen, remove and pack in plastic bags in the freezer. Use in cooking whenever chicken broth or bouillon is required.

1 soup chicken (fowl), about 4 pounds
2 quarts water
1 whole onion, peeled
4 whole carrots, scraped
4 stalks celery, including tops
1 parsnip root, scraped (optional)
2 sprigs parsley
2 sprigs dill
2 teaspoons salt
¼ teaspoon pepper

Clean chicken and wash well. Place in a deep pot, add water and remaining ingredients. Bring to a boil, then reduce heat and simmer, covered, until chicken is tender, about 2 hours. Remove chicken, strain soup, and chill. Skim off fat which rises and solidifies at the top. Discard all vegetables except the carrot which may be sliced and served in the soup. Chunks of chicken may also be served in the soup, if desired. Cook fine noodles or rice and add to soup, if desired.

Makes 8 servings.

———

NOTE: Soup chicken may be served separately as is, or may be chilled and cut up for chicken salad.

Cream of Leftover Vegetable Soup

SENSITIVITY CHECKLIST:

This recipe is   **dairy**   ____-free

     egg   ✓-free

     wheat   ✓-free

     corn   ✓-free

     sugar   ✓-free

If the child has been placed on a natural salicylate-free diet, do not use any soup with tomatoes in it until permission has been granted to do so. This is an easy recipe using frozen chicken broth cubes and leftover vegetables. Increase amounts if you wish to serve more. Add complimenting herbs, if desired.

½ cup chicken broth (see Index)
1 cup leftover cooked vegetables
¼ cup heavy cream
¼ teaspoon salt
Dash pepper

Place broth and vegetables in an electric blender; process until smooth. Pour into a saucepan. Add cream, salt and pepper. Heat but do not boil.

Makes 2 to 3 servings.

7

Meat

You don't have to give up interesting flavors when you're cooking for the hyperactive child and family, but you do have to watch the ingredients you use if there are any special restrictions. Don't feel that you have to serve plain broiled steaks, chops, and hamburgers; that can get boring even when you plan a good rotation menu that alternates with servings of poultry and fish. The better way is to learn new techniques of preparing familiar cuts of meat.

This chapter is filled with ways to enhance the flavor of the meats you are already using. It has many recipes for the less expensive cuts too. But low price should not always be the determining factor when choosing a cut of meat. There is less actual meat in cuts that have a large quantity of bone and fat. A good rule-of-thumb guide when choosing how much to buy for an adequate portion of meat for one person is:

⅓ pound of boneless meat
½ pound of meat with small amount of bone
1 pound of meat with large amount of bone

The most expensive cuts of beef are also the tenderest. They come from the loin, rib, and sirloin sections of the animal. Other cuts are less tender and require longer cooking and braising, unless they are marinated for several hours before cooking.

Quality beef is generally bright red in color with firm, finely grained fresh and well-marbled streaks of white fat. Beef is graded U.S. Prime, U.S. Choice, and U.S. Good for most home use. U.S. Prime is the finest meat available and the most expensive. U.S. Choice is the grade that is most available in supermarkets: it has less fat and is more tender than the lower quality of U.S. Good.

Veal, being the meat of a young calf, has little fat graining, but the color of the meat usually tells the story. Look for veal that is pinkish-white in color; avoid the older grayed-out or getting-red colors. What fat there is should be white and firm, and the bone marrow should look young and porous.

When buying lamb, look for pale pink lean meat as it is a sign of a young milk-fed animal. The color darkens with age and becomes known as mutton when the animal reaches 20 months old. The fat should be a waxy white and firm to the touch. Unless you prefer lamb that is well done, you need not serve it that way but can serve it pink instead.

Pork covers a multitude of cuts and curing techniques used for the meat of the hog. When buying fresh pork look for a gray-pink to rose color, and again look for firm white fat. Cook fresh pork at least 30 minutes to the pound to be sure that no pink remains in the center of the meat. It's the best way to destroy any organisms that may be unhealthy for you and to bring out the fullest flavor of the meat. A canned, fully cooked ham does not need any further cooking, unless you wish to bake it "Virginia style" or use it as the base of another cooked dish. Read labels of canned hams carefully to determine whether they should be eaten by the hyperactive child.

Fresh meat should be loosely wrapped and can be stored in the refrigerator for several days. Ground meat should be used within a day or two. Read the labels on cured and smoked meats. They should be wrapped and stored in the refrigerator and used within a week. Frozen meat should be wrapped airtight and placed in the freezer immediately after purchase. All frozen meat should be stored at 0°F. or lower. It should not be refrozen after defrosting unless you have cooked it; then it may be refrozen once. Frozen meat should not be allowed to defrost unless it is to be cooked promptly. You may keep ground meat in the freezer from 1 to 3 months; fresh pork from 3 to 6 months; lamb and veal from 6 to 9 months; and beef from 6 to 12 months.

If your child is to be kept on a rotation diet, refrain from serving him leftovers for lunch or dinner. Leftovers may be served to other members of the family. Do not repeat any one food more often than once every four days.

When dining out, if the child has been placed on a natural salicylate-free diet, keep a careful watch to be sure that nothing is ordered that has been cooked with tomatoes, mint, or cloves. Order the simplest of foods that could not have been prepared with any convenience food product. If there is a sensitivity to corn, do not order any fried foods for the child as you will not be able to determine what kind of oil has been used or what kinds of food have been submerged in the restaurant's deep fryer.

Here are a bevy of delicious meat dishes that should please everyone in the family. Read the notes before each recipe to guide you in your choices.

Swiss Steak

SENSITIVITY CHECKLIST:

This recipe is  __✓__-free

__✓__-free

_____-free

__✓__-free

__✓__-free

Here's a novel way to cook Swiss steak for the child who is on a natural salicylate-free diet. Cook over low heat for greatest tenderness.

2-pound slice of top round steak
2 tablespoons flour
½ teaspoon salt
¼ teaspoon pepper
3 tablespoons olive oil
1 onion, sliced
1 cup grapefruit juice

Combine flour, salt, and pepper; pound mixture into surface of steak on all sides. In a Dutch oven, heat the oil. Add onion slices and cook until golden. Add prepared round steak and brown on all sides. Pour grapefruit juice around steak; cover and cook for 1 hour, or until tender.

Makes 6 servings.

Gourmet Steak

SENSITIVITY CHECKLIST:

This recipe is _____-free (dairy)

✓-free (egg)

✓-free (wheat)

✓-free (corn)

✓-free (sugar)

The difference between a good steak and a great steak is sometimes just a few gourmet tricks. Try this recipe on the outdoor grill too.

½ teaspoon dry mustard
½ teaspoon water
1 tablespoon Worcestershire sauce
2 tablespoons butter, melted
1 sirloin steak, about 2 to 3 pounds
½ teaspoon salt
⅛ teaspoon pepper

Mix mustard with water and let it stand 10 minutes. Combine with Worcestershire sauce and melted butter. Broil steak on one side, turn and make several shallow slashes across top of steak. Pour butter mixture over steak and complete broiling. Season with salt and pepper and serve at once.

Makes 4 to 6 servings.

Flank Steak with Chive Butter

SENSITIVITY CHECKLIST:

This recipe is ⬚ _____-free
dairy

🥚 __✓_-free
egg

🌾 __✓_-free
wheat

🌽 __✓_-free
corn

🥣 __✓_-free
sugar

The trick to slicing a flank steak properly is to angle the knife almost parallel with the steak, cutting across the grain in broad strips. If Dijon mustard is unavailable, stir a bit of pure distilled vinegar into powdered mustard and use as a substitute.

1 flank steak, about 2 pounds
1 teaspoon pure Dijon mustard
2 tablespoons butter, melted
1 teaspoon chopped chives

Place flank steak on a broiling pan; spread a thin coating of mustard over top of steak. Broil for 5 to 6 minutes; turn and broil on the other side for an additional 5 to 6 minutes or until done as desired. Combine melted butter and chives; pour over steak just before serving. To serve, slice very thinly on the diagonal, across the grain of the meat.

Makes 4 servings.

Swiss Stuffed Flank Steak

SENSITIVITY CHECKLIST:

This recipe is   ___✓___-free

dairy

   ___✓___-free

egg

   ___✓___-free

wheat

   _____-free

corn

   _____-free

sugar

If child has been placed on a corn-free regime, substitute any other vegetable oil and use flour instead of cornstarch. If child is on a natural salicylate-free diet, do not use this stuffing until permission has been granted to resume the use of apples and prunes.

1 flank steak, 1½ to 2 pounds
Salt
Pepper
¼ cup finely chopped onion
2 apples, peeled, cored, and sliced
8 pitted prunes
2 tablespoons corn oil
1 cup water
1½ cups apple juice
2 tablespoons cornstarch
1 teaspoon salt
1 tablespoon brown sugar
¼ teaspoon onion powder

Trim excess fat and membrane from steak. Score both sides and sprinkle with salt and pepper. Pound both sides with meat mallet. Sprinkle one side with onion; arrange apples and prunes in center across short side of steak. Fold in thirds and tie securely. In Dutch oven or large skillet heat corn oil over medium heat. Add steak; brown on all sides. Reduce heat; add water. Cover and simmer 1 hour or until meat is fork tender. Remove meat; keep warm. Gradually stir apple juice into cornstarch until smooth. Stir into pan juices. Stir in 1 teaspoon salt, brown sugar, and onion powder. Cook over medium heat, stirring constantly, until mixture thickens and comes to a boil. Serve gravy over meat.

Makes 6 servings.

Rice Stuffed Flank Steak

SENSITIVITY CHECKLIST:

This recipe is   _✓_-free   dairy

_____-free   egg

_✓_-free   wheat

_____-free   corn

_✓_-free   sugar

If child has been placed on a corn-free regime, substitute any other vegetable oil and use flour instead of cornstarch.

1½ cups cooked rice
1 egg, slightly beaten
2 tablespoons chopped parsley
1 teaspoon salt
1 flank steak, about 2 pounds
¼ cup corn oil
4 cups beef stock or water
1 teaspoon dried oregano leaves
1 pound green beans, trimmed
1 pound mushrooms
3 tablespoons cornstarch
¼ cup water

Stir together rice, egg, and parsley. Sprinkle salt over steak. Spread rice mixture over steak to within 1 inch of edge. Roll up and tie securely with string. In 5-quart Dutch oven heat corn oil over medium heat. Add steak; brown well on all sides. Add beef stock and oregano. Cover; bring to boil. Reduce heat; simmer 1 hour and 15 minutes. Add beans and mushrooms; continue cooking 20 minutes or until vegetables are tender crisp. Remove steak and vegetables to platter; keep warm. Stir together cornstarch and water until smooth. Stir into pan juices in Dutch oven. Bring to boil over medium heat, stirring constantly; boil 1 minute. Serve gravy with steak.

Makes 6 to 8 servings.

Flank Steak Teriyaki

SENSITIVITY CHECKLIST:

This recipe is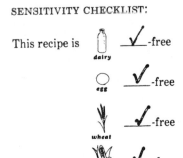

dairy ___✓___-free

egg ___✓___-free

wheat ___✓___-free

corn ___✓___-free

sugar _____-free

Brown sugar may be eliminated if child is on a sugar-free regime. If allowed, a teaspoon of honey may be substituted. Think of this recipe when you are barbecuing outdoors.

1 flank steak, about 2 pounds
¼ cup pure soy sauce
1 tablespoon brown sugar
½ teaspoon ginger
1 clove crushed garlic
1 tablespoon salad oil

Place flank steak on a broiling rack. Combine soy sauce, brown sugar, ginger, garlic, and oil. Brush half this mixture on top of steak. Broil 10 minutes. Turn and brush remaining sauce on top of steak. Broil 5 to 10 minutes more, depending on desired degree of rareness. Slice steak on a wide angle.

Makes 4 servings.

Pot Roast

SENSITIVITY CHECKLIST:

This recipe is dairy __✓__-free

egg __✓__-free

wheat __✓__-free

corn ____-free

sugar __✓__-free

If child has been placed on a corn-free regime, substitute any other vegetable oil and use flour instead of cornstarch.

¼ cup corn oil
1 boneless beef pot roast, about 4 to 5 pounds
2 cups chopped onion
2½ cups beef stock or water
2 teaspoons salt
1 teaspoon pepper
2 crushed bay leaves
8 small potatoes, peeled
1 pound whole green beans
⅓ cup cornstarch
⅓ cup water

In Dutch oven or large kettle heat corn oil over medium heat. Add meat. Brown on all sides. Stir in onion, beef stock, salt, pepper, and bay leaves. Cover. Bake in 350° F. oven about 2½ hours or until meat is almost tender. Add potatoes. Cover and cook ½ hour or until meat and potatoes are tender. Add green beans. Cover and cook an additional 10 to 15 minutes or until beans are tender crisp. Remove meat and vegetables to platter. Stir together cornstarch and water until smooth. Add to liquid in Dutch oven. Bring to a boil over medium heat, stirring constantly, and boil 1 minute. Serve gravy over meat and vegetables.

Makes about 8 servings.

Baked Brisket

SENSITIVITY CHECKLIST:

This recipe is ✔-free
dairy

✔-free
egg

✔-free
wheat

✔-free
corn

✔-free
sugar

The trick to making delicious brisket is to cook it long on low heat. If time permits, lower oven heat to 250°F. and cook an additional 30 minutes, or until tender.

4 pounds brisket of beef
½ teaspoon salt
¼ teaspoon pepper
½ teaspoon paprika
2 onions, thinly sliced
2 cups water
2 bay leaves
4 scraped carrots, thinly sliced
4 potatoes, peeled and quartered

Place brisket in a Dutch oven; season with salt, pepper, and paprika. Cover with sliced onions. Pour water around the brisket. Add bay leaves and sliced carrots. Cover and bake in a 325° F. oven for 2 hours. Add potatoes and continue baking, covered, for an additional 30 minutes to 1 hour or until brisket and potatoes are tender. Remove bay leaves. Slice brisket and serve with potatoes and gravy.

Makes 8 to 10 servings.

Sauerbraten

SENSITIVITY CHECKLIST:

This recipe is   **dairy**   ✓ -free

egg   ✓ -free

wheat   _____ -free

corn   ✓ -free

sugar   _____ -free

This dish has a tangy sweet and sour flavor. It is delicious served with cooked red cabbage and potato pancakes.

4-pound beef roast, round or brisket
2 cups white vinegar
1 cup water
1 tablespoon sugar
1 teaspoon ginger
2 bay leaves
6 whole peppercorns
2 onions, sliced
½ cup flour
½ cup oil

In a saucepan, heat vinegar, water, sugar, ginger, bay leaves, peppercorns, and onions for 10 minutes. Cool. Place meat in a large deep bowl and cover with the cooled mixture. Refrigerate for 2 days, turning meat morning and night. Remove meat from marinade and wipe dry. Pat with flour. Brown in oil on all sides. Place meat in a Dutch oven and add 1 cup of the marinade. Simmer, covered, for 2 to 2½ hours, until meat is tender. Remove and slice. Serve with gravy.

Makes 8 servings.

Roast Sirloin of Beef

SENSITIVITY CHECKLIST:

This recipe is   ___✔___-free
                    dairy

                    ___✔___-free
                    egg

                    _____-free
                    wheat

                    ___✔___-free
                    corn

                    ___✔___-free
                    sugar

If child is sensitive to wheat, flour may be omitted from this recipe. Chill leftovers and slice thinly with a food slicer or an electric knife for maximum quantity.

1 teaspoon salt
½ teaspoon onion salt
½ teaspoon paprika
2 tablespoons flour
1 sirloin beef roast, about 4 pounds

Combine salt, onion salt, paprika, and flour; pat mixture all over surface of roast. Place on a rack in a shallow roasting pan. Place in a preheated 350° F. oven and roast for about 20 minutes to the pound for rare, 25 minutes for medium, 30 minutes for well done. Remove roast to platter to rest before carving. For a quick pan gravy, pour a cup of boiling water into the pan of drippings; scrape and stir. Then heat on top of the range. Strain before serving, if preferred.

Makes 6 to 8 servings.

Beef Stew

SENSITIVITY CHECKLIST:

This recipe is

If child is sensitive to natural salicylates, omit tomatoes and tomato sauce from recipe. Substitute 3 cups of water and add other fresh vegetables if desired.

2 pounds lean beef, cut into cubes
½ cup flour
2 teaspoons salt
⅛ teaspoon pepper
¼ cup cooking oil
2 onions, sliced
1 clove garlic, diced
1 can (16 ounces) whole tomatoes in natural juice
1 can (8 ounces) pure tomato sauce
1 small bunch of celery, trimmed and cut into 1-inch chunks
8 carrots, scraped and cut into 1-inch chunks
½ pound fresh small mushrooms
6 potatoes, pared and quartered
2 bay leaves

Dredge beef cubes in a mixture of flour, 1 teaspoon salt, and pepper. Heat oil in a Dutch oven; sauté onions and garlic until limp. Add beef cubes and brown on all sides. Stir in tomatoes and tomato sauce. Add celery, carrots, mushrooms, and potatoes. Season with the remaining 1 teaspoon of salt. Add bay leaves. Simmer on top of range 2 hours or until meat is tender. Discard bay leaves and serve.

Makes 6 to 8 servings.

Fluffy Meat Loaf

SENSITIVITY CHECKLIST:

This recipe is   ✓ -free (dairy)

_____ -free (egg)

_____ -free (wheat)

✓ -free (corn)

✓ -free (sugar)

This meat loaf mixture can be prepared and frozen uncooked in a loaf pan. To cook, place frozen meat loaf in 350°F. oven and bake for 1¾ hours. Or thaw in refrigerator for a day and bake as directed below. If bread has milk or butter listed as an ingredient, it will not be dairy-free.

2 pounds ground beef
2 eggs
2 slices natural bread
½ cup cold water
1 small potato, peeled and grated
¼ cup chopped parsley
2 tablespoons minced onion
1 teaspoon salt
¼ teaspoon pepper

Combine ground beef and eggs. Soak bread in water and shred. Add to meat with grated potato; mix well. Add parsley, onion, salt, and pepper. Turn into a 9-by-5-by-3-inch loaf pan, or form into a loaf shape in a shallow baking pan. Bake in a preheated 350° F. oven for 1 hour.

Makes 8 servings.

Oatmeal Meat Loaf

SENSITIVITY CHECKLIST:

This recipe is

_____-free

_____-free

___✓-free.

___✓-free

___✓-free

If the child is on a dairy-free diet, water may be substituted for the milk. Tomato juice may also be substituted for the milk if the child is not on a natural salicylate-free diet.

1½ pounds ground beef
¾ cup uncooked Quaker Oats
1 egg, beaten
1 small onion, chopped
¾ teaspoon salt
¼ teaspoon pepper
¼ teaspoon garlic powder
½ cup milk

Mix ground beef, cereal, egg, and onion together. Add salt, pepper, and garlic powder. Work in milk until all is mixed well. Pack into a loaf pan and bake in a 350° F. oven for 1 hour.

Makes 4 to 6 servings.

Chili-Beef on Rice

SENSITIVITY CHECKLIST:

This recipe is   ___✓___-free
                  dairy

                  ___✓___-free
                  egg

                  ___✓___-free
                  wheat

                  ___✓___-free
                  corn

                  ___✓___-free
                  sugar

If child has been placed on a natural salicylate-free diet, omit this recipe until permission has been granted to add tomatoes to the child's diet.

1½ pounds ground beef
1 tablespoon cooking oil
1 cup chopped onions
1 cup finely diced green pepper
1 teaspoon salt
1 teaspoon chili powder
⅛ teaspoon pepper
1 can (16 ounces) tomatoes in natural juices
3 cups cooked rice

Brown beef in oil; then add onions and green pepper. Cook until onions are limp, mixing with a fork. Add salt, chili powder, and pepper. Stir in tomatoes. Cover and simmer about 35 minutes, stirring occasionally to break up the tomatoes. Serve over hot cooked rice.

Makes 6 servings.

Western Hash

SENSITIVITY CHECKLIST:

This recipe is [dairy] ✓-free

[egg] ✓-free

[wheat] ✓-free

[corn] ✓-free

[sugar] ✓-free

If child has been placed on natural salicylate-free diet, omit recipe until advised by your doctor to resume the use of tomatoes for your child.

2 tablespoons cooking oil
¼ cup finely chopped onion
¼ cup chopped green pepper
1 pound ground beef
1 teaspoon salt
1 teaspoon chili powder
¼ cup pure molasses
¼ cup pure Dijon mustard
2 tablespoons pure Worcestershire sauce
1 can (16 ounces) tomatoes in natural juice
¼ cup chopped ripe olives
1 cup uncooked regular rice

Heat oil in a large skillet. Add onion and green pepper and cook until onion is tender but not brown. Add ground beef, ½ teaspoon salt, and chili powder. Brown beef, breaking up into pieces with a fork. While beef is browning, mix molasses and mustard. Stir in Worcestershire sauce. Add to the beef mixture with tomatoes, olives, and the remaining ½ teaspoon salt. Gradually add rice. Cover; reduce heat and simmer 25 to 30 minutes or until rice is tender.

Makes 4 servings.

Spicy Meatballs

SENSITIVITY CHECKLIST:

This recipe is   *✓*-free   dairy

_____-free   egg

_____-free   wheat

✓-free   corn

✓-free   sugar

The meatballs may be formed in advance and frozen uncooked. Or cook meatballs as directed in recipe and freeze in the sauce.

2 pounds ground beef
1 onion, finely chopped
1 cup fine bread crumbs (see Index)
2 eggs
¼ cup grated Parmesan cheese
¾ teaspoon curry powder
½ teaspoon salt
¼ teaspoon pepper
½ teaspoon pure Worcestershire sauce
2 cloves garlic, diced
1 cup flour
2 tablespoons olive oil
1 cup water
2 cans (8 ounces) pure tomato sauce
¼ teaspoon oregano

Combine ground beef, onion, and bread crumbs. Add eggs, cheese, curry powder, salt, pepper, and Worcestershire sauce. Add half of the diced garlic and mix well. Form mixture into 1½-inch balls. Roll each ball lightly in the flour. Heat oil and the remaining diced garlic in a large skillet; add meatballs and brown on all sides. Remove meatballs when browned. Stir water, tomato sauce, and oregano into the skillet. Mix the remaining flour with a little water to form a thin paste and stir into the tomato mixture. Add the meatballs; cover and simmer about 25 minutes.

Makes 8 servings.

Beef-Noodle Skillet

SENSITIVITY CHECKLIST:

This recipe is   ✓-free (dairy)

_____-free (egg)

_____-free (wheat)

✓-free (corn)

✓-free (sugar)

If child has been placed on a natural salicylate-free diet, omit this recipe until advised by your doctor to resume the use of tomatoes.

1 can (8 ounces) pure tomato sauce
½ cup water
1⅔ tablespoons salt
¼ teaspoon coarsely ground black pepper
1½ teaspoons oregano
¼ teaspoon thyme
1 teaspoon pure Worcestershire sauce
3 tablespoons cooking oil
1 pound ground beef chuck
1¼ cups chopped onions
1 clove garlic, crushed
1 medium green pepper, diced
2 cups sliced celery
½ cup chopped parsley
3 quarts boiling water
1 package (8 ounces) wide egg noodles (no artificial color)

Combine tomato sauce, ½ cup water, 2 teaspoons salt, pepper, oregano, thyme, and Worcestershire sauce; set aside. Heat oil in a large skillet over medium heat; add beef and stir constantly until browned. Remove meat with a slotted spoon and set aside. Sauté onions, garlic, green pepper, and celery in the drippings in skillet until crisp and tender. Cover and cook over low heat about 6 to 8 minutes longer, stirring occasionally, until tender. Drain. Cook noodles in boiling water with 1 tablespoon salt. Drain. Add the reserved meat, tomato sauce mixture, and hot cooked noodles to vegetables in skillet; toss lightly until combined. Heat through.

Makes 4 servings.

Cheese Muffin-Burgers

SENSITIVITY CHECKLIST:

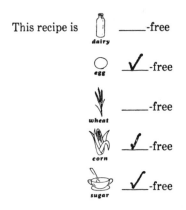

This recipe is ____-free

_____-free (egg)

____-free (wheat)

____-free (corn)

____-free (sugar)

If child has been placed on a natural salicylate-free diet, omit this recipe until permission has been given to include apples in the diet. If sensitive to dairy products, omit cheese topping.

1½ pounds ground beef
1½ cups bread crumbs (see Index)
1 teaspoon minced onion
1 teaspoon salt
½ teaspoon dry mustard
1 cup applesauce (no artificial additives)
3 slices white cheddar cheese, cut in quarters

Combine ground beef, bread crumbs, onion, salt, and mustard in a large bowl. Add the applesauce and mix thoroughly with a wooden spoon. Let stand until the applesauce has moistened the ingredients thoroughly. Divide the meat mixture into 12 equal portions and pack into ungreased muffin cups. Bake in a preheated 350° F. oven for 15 to 20 minutes. Top each muffin-burger with a cheese wedge; return to oven until cheese is slightly melted.

Makes 12 burgers.

Herbed Hamburgers

SENSITIVITY CHECKLIST:

This recipe is

dairy ___✓-free

egg ___✓-free

wheat ___✓-free

corn ___✓-free

sugar ___✓-free

For a change of pace, this hamburger has a different flavor and is egg-free and wheat-free. If neither of these sensitivities trouble the hyperactive child, egg and bread crumbs may be used in this recipe to stretch the meat servings.

1 pound ground beef
2 tablespoons grated onion
1 teaspoon pure soy sauce
½ teaspoon salt
¼ teaspoon pepper
¼ teaspoon marjoram
¼ teaspoon thyme

Combine all ingredients and form into 4 hamburgers. Broil about 10 minutes, depending on degree of rareness desired.

Makes 4 servings.

Veal Parmigiana

SENSITIVITY CHECKLIST:

This recipe is   _____-free
    dairy

    _____-free
    egg

    _____-free
    wheat

    _✓_-free
    corn

    _✓_-free
    sugar

If child has been placed on a natural salicylate-free diet, remove one portion to a separate baking dish before pouring tomato sauce over veal. If child is sensitive to dairy products, omit cheese on one portion.

1½ pounds thinly sliced veal
1 egg, beaten
½ cup fine bread crumbs (see Index)
¼ cup cooking oil
1 can (16 ounces) tomato sauce (no artificial additives)
1 teaspoon oregano
8 ounces sliced mozzarella cheese
2 tablespoons grated Parmesan cheese

Dip each slice of veal into the beaten egg and then into bread crumbs, coating thoroughly. Heat oil in a skillet and brown veal slices on both sides. When well browned, remove from skillet and place in a flat baking dish. Pour tomato sauce over veal. Sprinkle with oregano. Top veal slices with a slice of mozzarella cheese; sprinkle Parmesan cheese over all. Bake in a preheated 350° F. oven for 25 minutes or until cheese is melted and lightly browned.

Makes 6 servings.

Veal Pot Roast

SENSITIVITY CHECKLIST:

This recipe is

dairy ✓-free

egg ✓-free

wheat ✓-free

corn ✓-free

sugar ✓-free

No harm done if you add a few peeled and quartered potatoes with the carrots to make it a one-pot meal. Dried dill may be substituted for fresh dill, if necessary.

1 boned and tied veal shoulder roast, about 3 pounds
1 clove garlic, cut in half
1 tablespoon paprika
1 teaspoon salt
¼ teaspoon pepper
3 tablespoons cooking oil
1 onion, diced
1 cup water
Sprig of fresh dill
4 carrots, scraped and cut into 2-inch chunks

Rub veal roast with cut sides of garlic; reserve garlic. Combine paprika, salt, and pepper; rub all over surface of roast. Heat oil in a deep kettle or Dutch oven; sauté onion until lightly golden. Add reserved garlic to oil. Add veal and brown on all sides. Remove garlic. Add water, dill, and carrots. Cover and simmer 1½ hours (about 30 minutes to the pound).

Makes 6 to 8 servings.

Breast of Veal with Rice Stuffing

SENSITIVITY CHECKLIST:

This recipe is   ✓-free

✓-free

✓-free

✓-free

✓-free

This inexpensive cut of meat gives a lot of good taste. Fun to nibble on the bones too!

1 breast of veal, about 4 pounds
2 cups cooked rice
2 tablespoons minced parsley
1 teaspoon grated lemon rind
½ teaspoon basil
½ teaspoon salt
⅛ teaspoon pepper
½ teaspoon paprika
¼ teaspoon garlic salt

Have butcher slit a pocket into the breast of veal for stuffing. Combine cooked rice, parsley, lemon rind, basil, salt, and pepper. Stuff into veal pocket. Place breast of veal in a roasting pan; sprinkle surface with paprika and garlic salt. Roast in a 350° F. oven for 2 to 2½ hours, or until brown and tender.

Makes 6 servings.

Roast Leg of Lamb

SENSITIVITY CHECKLIST:

This recipe is  __✓__-free *dairy*

__✓__-free *egg*

__✓__-free *wheat*

__✓__-free *corn*

__✓__-free *sugar*

If the child is placed on a natural salicylate-free diet, be sure that vinegar is the plain white distilled variety. Grapes used in making wine vinegar and apples used in making cider vinegar are both on the salicylate list of foods to be eliminated.

1 leg of lamb roast, about 5 pounds
1 clove garlic, minced
1 teaspoon salt
¼ teaspoon pepper
½ teaspoon paprika
½ teaspoon rosemary
1 onion, finely diced
2 tablespoons white vinegar
¼ cup olive oil

Rub lamb with a mixture of garlic, salt, pepper, paprika, and rosemary. Place on a rack in a roasting pan. Combine onion, vinegar, and oil; pour over lamb. Place in a preheated 350° F. oven and roast for about 20 minutes to the pound for rare, 25 minutes for medium, 30 minutes for well done. Let roast stand for 15 minutes (it will carve more easily).

Makes 6 to 8 servings.

Lamb Shanks

SENSITIVITY CHECKLIST:

This recipe is

dairy ___✓__-free

egg ___✓__-free

wheat ___✓__-free

corn ___✓__-free

sugar ___✓__-free

If child has been placed on a natural salicylate-free diet, use grapefruit juice instead of orange juice, until permission has been granted to resume the use of orange juice.

4 lamb shanks
1 cup orange juice
2 tablespoons butter
1 tablespoon chopped parsley
½ teaspoon salt
½ teaspoon rosemary

Arrange lamb shanks in a small roasting pan. In a small saucepan, combine orange juice, butter, parsley, salt, and rosemary; heat and stir until butter melts. Brush half the mixture over the lamb shanks. Roast 1 hour in a 350° F. oven, basting occasionally with remaining sauce. Continue roasting until fork tender.

Makes 4 servings.

Lamb Chops Italienne

This recipe is  ✓-free

✓-free

✓-free

✓-free

✓-free

Be sure to avoid the use of wine vinegar if the child has been placed on a natural salicylate-free diet. If desired, lamb chops may marinate in vinegar mixture for an hour before broiling, turning frequently to coat well.

6 large shoulder lamb chops
¼ cup white vinegar
2 tablespoons lemon juice
1 tablespoon olive oil
1 clove garlic, crushed
¾ teaspoon oregano
½ teaspoon salt
¼ teaspoon pepper

Arrange lamb chops on a rack in a broiling pan. Combine vinegar, lemon juice, olive oil, garlic, oregano, salt, and pepper; brush mixture on chops and broil for about 8 minutes. Turn chops, brush remaining mixture on other side and broil until done to your taste.

Makes 4 to 6 servings.

Yogurt Lamb Kebobs

SENSITIVITY CHECKLIST:

This recipe is ⬜ _____-free

dairy

○ ✔-free

egg

🌾 ✔-free

wheat

🌽 ✔-free

corn

☕ ✔-free

sugar

Don't skip the marinating time. It makes the difference between ordinary kebobs and tender flavorful ones.

1 cup plain yogurt
1 tablespoon lemon juice
2 tablespoons grated onion
1 teaspoon minced fresh dill
½ teaspoon salt
2 pounds cubed lamb
8 small onions, boiled
8 mushroom caps
2 tablespoons melted butter

Combine yogurt, lemon juice, onion, dill, and salt. Stir in lamb cubes; marinate in refrigerator for several hours. Skewer lamb cubes, onions, and mushroom caps. Place in a flat pan. Brush with half the melted butter. Broil 6 minutes. Turn and brush with remaining melted butter; broil 6 minutes more or until tender.

Makes 4 servings.

Irish Stew

This recipe is ____✓____-free dairy

____✓____-free egg

____✓____-free wheat

____✓____-free corn

____✓____-free sugar

Add other vegetables as the spirit moves you. However, if the child is on a natural salicylate-free diet do not add tomatoes unless permission has been granted to use them.

2 pounds cubed lamb
2 large onions, sliced
2 tablespoons cooking oil
2 tablespoons minced parsley
1 teaspoon salt
¼ teaspoon pepper
1½ cups water
4 large potatoes, cut in chunks
4 carrots, scraped and cut in chunks
2 stalks celery, cut in chunks

Brown lamb cubes and onions in oil in a large heavy saucepan. Add parsley, salt, and pepper. Add water. Cover and simmer for 1 hour until tender. Add potatoes, carrots, and celery; cover and simmer for ½ hour longer or until tender.

Makes 4 servings.

Pineapple Pepper Pork Chops

SENSITIVITY CHECKLIST:

This recipe is

✔-free

dairy

✔-free

egg

✔-free

wheat

_____-free

corn

✔-free

sugar

If child has been placed on a corn-free regime, substitute any other vegetable oil and use flour instead of cornstarch.

2 tablespoons corn oil
4 pork chops, 1 inch thick
1 can (8 ounces) sliced pineapple or pineapple chunks with juice
1 tablespoon natural soy sauce
¼ teaspoon dried thyme
½ teaspoon salt
¼ teaspoon pepper
2 tablespoons cornstarch
½ cup beef stock or chicken broth (see Index)
¼ cup chopped green pepper
4 green pepper rings

In skillet heat corn oil over medium heat. Add pork chops. Brown on all sides. Place chops in a shallow baking dish. Mix together pineapple juice, soy sauce, thyme, salt, and pepper. Stir together cornstarch and beef stock until smooth. Stir into pineapple juice mixture. Pour over pork chops. Add chopped green pepper. Cover. Bake in 350° F. oven 45 minutes or until pork chops are tender. Remove from oven. Top pork chops with pineapple pieces and green pepper rings. Continue baking, uncovered, 5 minutes or until pineapple is heated through and gravy thickened.

Makes 4 servings.

8

Poultry

Poultry is economical, high in nutrition, and extremely adaptable to a variety of cooking techniques. And there's a wide range of birds from which to choose, including chickens, ducklings, Rock Cornish hens, and turkeys.

If the different designations of chickens confuse you, try to remember that they generally reflect the age and size of the bird. Younger birds are called "broilers" or "fryers" and they are best cooked as their label suggests. However, if they are meaty enough, you can roast or pot these young birds. Heavy fowl is more desirable to use for stews and soups, as it is meatier and has a more definite flavor, being an older chicken.

Ducklings generally are obtainable in the four- to six-pound range, with each duck serving two to four people, depending on the meatiness of the bird. Ducks are very fatty and are best cooked by roasting in a very hot oven on a rack over a pan for the first half hour. Prick the skin with a fork several times to permit the fat to drain out as it melts. Then lower the heat to 350° F. and cook until fork tender.

Rock Cornish hens are available in single serving size up to one pound each, or in larger sizes to be split in half after cooking. For best results, thaw the frozen hens before seasoning and cooking.

When choosing a turkey for roasting, keep in mind that the bone structure stops growing at about the ten-pound size, so every pound over that is proportionately more meat and less bone for the price. You may prefer to buy a small boneless turkey roast, but be sure to check the label to be sure that it has not been prepared with any artificial additives. If there is a hyperactive child in the family, do not choose any of the large turkeys that have been prestuffed, or the self-basting variety. The best way to roast a turkey is "low and slow." After cleaning and seasoning the bird, place it in a large roasting pan and tent a piece of aluminum foil over the top. Place the bird in a 325° F. oven for approximately the following time schedule:

```
 6 to  8 pound turkey—roasting time is 3 to 3½ hours
 8 to 12 pound turkey—roasting time is 3½ to 4½ hours
12 to 16 pound turkey—roasting time is 4½ to 5½ hours
16 to 20 pound turkey—roasting time is 5½ to 6½ hours
20 to 24 pound turkey—roasting time is 6½ to 7 hours
```

Raw poultry may be kept in the refrigerator for one or two days if all plastic wrappings have been removed and the poultry is wrapped loosely in waxed paper.

Never leave stuffing in poultry if you are storing it in the refrigerator to use again. The cold of the refrigerator may not penetrate to the center of the bird, and you are courting bacteria growth by leaving the stuffing in the bird. To be safe remove it and store it separately in a covered container.

The same rule of thumb applies to poultry as it does to meat: you may freeze it once raw and once cooked. After cooking, the poultry should be frozen in broth or gravy because it will be tastier when reheated.

It's a good idea to have several single portions of poultry cooked and frozen, in case the family is planning to enjoy a meal that the hyperactive child is not permitted to have. It's not the ideal situation but one that may realistically happen now and then. If you have something special that the child loves, it won't matter as much.

Again, avoid foods cooked with tomatoes or other natural salicylates if the child has been placed on this regime. Don't hesitate to warn any hostess entertaining the child that a condition exists that requires a diet free of artificial additives, and that you would appreciate it if the child is served food within those limitations. No need to discuss it further as many people are into natural foods these days as a way of life for the whole family.

You'll find a number of tasty poultry dishes in this chapter to add to those your family already enjoys.

Chicken and Cashews

SENSITIVITY CHECKLIST:

This recipe is ☐ ✓-free (dairy)

◯ ✓-free (egg)

🌾 ✓-free (wheat)

🌽 ____-free (corn)

🥣 ✓-free (sugar)

Here's an Oriental dish that's bound to become a favorite at your house. Serve with pure soy sauce if desired.

2 tablespoons pure soy sauce
2 tablespoons water
2 teaspoons cornstarch
¼ teaspoon white pepper
2 whole chicken breasts, skinned, boned, and diced (1½ cups)
3 tablespoons corn oil
3 ounces whole mushrooms, sliced
½ cup diced green pepper
½ cup diced red pepper
1 tablespoon cornstarch
½ cup chicken stock (see Index)
¾ cup salted cashews
2 cups cooked rice

Stir together soy sauce, water, 2 teaspoons cornstarch and white pepper until smooth. Mix in chicken. Marinate ½ hour at room temperature. In wok or 4-quart saucepan, heat corn oil over medium high heat. Add mushrooms and peppers. Cook over high heat, stirring constantly, 1 minute. Remove and set aside. Add chicken to the corn oil. Cook over high heat, stirring constantly, 2 minutes or until tender. Stir together 1 tablespoon cornstarch and chicken stock. Add to wok. Bring to a boil over medium heat, stirring constantly, and boil 1 minute. Stir in mushrooms and peppers. Cook until heated through. Spoon over bed of hot cooked rice. Top with cashews.

Makes 4 servings.

Chicken Grand-mère

This recipe is

dairy ✓ -free

egg ✓ -free

wheat ✓ -free

corn ___ -free

sugar ✓ -free

If the child is on a corn-free regime, substitute wheat flour for cornstarch. Extra broth may be frozen for future use.

2 chicken fryers, cut up
6 cups water
2 cups sliced celery stalks and leaves
¾ cup parsley sprigs
2 medium onions, sliced
2 teaspoons salt
1 bay leaf
¼ teaspoon thyme
6 tablespoons cornstarch
Cooked rice

Place chicken in a 6-quart kettle; cover with water. Add celery, parsley, onions, salt, bay leaf, and thyme. Cover; bring to a boil, reduce heat, and simmer 1¼ hours or until chicken is tender. Remove chicken and discard bones. Strain broth; measure 6 cups, adding boiling water if necessary. Return 5 cups broth to kettle; mix together remaining broth and cornstarch until smooth. Stir into broth in kettle. Bring to boil, stirring constantly, and boil 1 minute until mixture is slightly thickened. Add chicken and heat. Serve over rice in soup bowls.

Makes 8 servings.

Chicken Fricassee

SENSITIVITY CHECKLIST:

This recipe is ☐ _✓_-free
dairy

○ _✓_-free
egg

🌾 _✓_-free
wheat

🌽 _____-free
corn

🍜 _✓_-free
sugar

If the child has been placed on a corn-free regime, substitute wheat flour for cornstarch. Add tiny meatballs if desired.

1 broiler chicken, cut up
2 carrots, quartered
1 stalk celery, halved
1 medium onion
2 sprigs parsley
1½ teaspoons salt
¾ teaspoon dried thyme
⅛ teaspoon white pepper
5 cups water
⅓ cup cornstarch
Cooked rice
Chopped parsley (optional)

In large kettle place chicken, carrots, celery, onion, parsley sprigs, salt, thyme, and pepper. Add water. Bring to a boil; reduce heat, cover, and simmer 45 minutes or until chicken is fork tender. Strain broth; discarding vegetables. Return 4 cups broth to kettle. Stir together cornstarch and remaining broth until smooth. Stir into broth in kettle. Bring to a boil over medium heat, stirring constantly, and boil 1 minute. Add chicken and heat. Serve over rice in soup bowls. If desired, sprinkle with chopped parsley.

Makes 4 servings.

NOTE: To make creamy Chicken Fricassee substitute 2 cups milk for 2 cups broth when making sauce.

Oriental Broiled Chicken

SENSITIVITY CHECKLIST:

This recipe is   dairy ___✓___-free

egg ___✓___-free

wheat ___✓___-free

corn ___✓___-free

sugar ___✓___-free

If the child has been placed on a natural salicylate-free diet, use unsweetened grapefruit juice instead of orange juice in this recipe, until permission has been granted to resume the use of orange in the diet. If permission has been given to use honey, despite a sugar-free regime, this recipe may be used.

1 cup orange juice
¼ cup honey
¼ cup soy sauce
1 clove garlic, crushed
½ teaspoon powdered ginger
2 broiler chickens, quartered

Combine orange juice, honey, soy sauce, garlic, and ginger, stirring well until honey is dissolved. Arrange chicken quarters in a broiling pan. Pour half of the orange juice mixture over the chicken. Broil for 15 minutes. Turn chicken quarters and pour the remaining orange mixture over all. Broil for an additional 15 minutes or until chicken is tender.

Makes 8 servings.

Chicken Cacciatore

SENSITIVITY CHECKLIST:

This recipe is   __✓__-free
dairy

__✓__-free
egg

_____-free
wheat

__✓__-free
corn

__✓__-free
sugar

An easy way to dredge the chicken is to pop all dry ingredients into a plastic bag and then shake several pieces of chicken at a time to coat well. Some of the remaining flour mixture may be used to thicken gravy, if desired.

2 broiler chickens, cut into parts
½ cup flour
1 teaspoon salt
½ teaspoon paprika
¼ teaspoon garlic powder
⅛ teaspoon pepper
¼ cup olive oil
1 can (16 ounces) tomatoes in natural liquid
1 cup chicken broth (see Index)
2 sweet Italian peppers, seeded and finely diced
½ pound fresh mushrooms, sliced

Dredge each chicken part in a mixture of flour, salt, paprika, garlic, and pepper. Heat oil in a Dutch oven; brown chicken on all sides. Add tomatoes, chicken broth, peppers, and mushrooms. Cover and simmer over low heat 1 hour or until tender.

Makes 6 to 8 servings.

Brunswick Stew

SENSITIVITY CHECKLIST:

This recipe is

✔ -free *dairy*

✔ -free *egg*

✔ -free *wheat*

____ -free *corn*

✔ -free *sugar*

If child has been placed on a natural salicylate-free diet, omit this recipe until permission has been granted to resume the use of tomatoes. If there is a sensitivity to corn, omit corn from this recipe. Serve Brunswick Stew in soup bowls with plenty of hearty bread.

1 chicken, cut up, about 3 pounds
1½ cups water
1 onion, thinly sliced
1 can (1 pound) tomatoes in natural juice
1 teaspoon salt
¼ teaspoon pepper
2 potatoes, peeled and cut in chunks
1 can (12 ounces) whole corn niblets, drained
1 can (8 ounces) okra, drained
1 teaspoon pure Worcestershire sauce

Place chicken parts in a deep saucepan. Add water, onion, tomatoes, salt, and pepper. Simmer, covered, for 15 minutes. Add potatoes, corn, okra, and Worcestershire sauce. Simmer, covered, for 30 minutes more, or until chicken is tender.

Makes 4 servings.

Wheat-free Fried Chicken

SENSITIVITY CHECKLIST:

This recipe is ☐ __✓__-free
  dairy

○ _____-free
  egg

🌾 __✓__-free
  wheat

🌽 _____-free
  corn

🥣 __✓__-free
  sugar

Here's a delicious way to fry chicken that the whole family will enjoy when a sensitivity to wheat necessitates a change of coating.

1 fryer chicken, cut up
Salt
Pepper
2 eggs
1 tablespoon water
¾ cup cornstarch
2 cups corn oil

Sprinkle chicken with salt and pepper. Beat eggs and water until well mixed. Dip chicken into egg mixture, then into cornstarch, coating evenly. Dip into egg mixture again; drain off excess. Pour corn oil into a large deep skillet to a depth of about ¼ inch. Heat over medium heat. Carefully put chicken into hot oil to avoid spattering. Cook, turning once, 25 to 30 minutes or until light golden brown and tender. Drain on absorbent paper.

Makes 4 servings.

Baked Lemon Chicken

SENSITIVITY CHECKLIST:

This recipe is ____-free *dairy*

✔-free *egg*

✔-free *wheat*

✔-free *corn*

✔-free *sugar*

Chicken and lemon have a natural affinity for each other. Try this combination for a truly yummy dish.

2 broiler chickens, cut in parts
3 tablespoons melted butter
⅓ cup lemon juice
1 tablespoon chopped fresh dill
½ teaspoon salt
½ teaspoon paprika

Arrange chicken in a flat baking dish. Combine the butter, lemon juice, dill, salt, and paprika; pour over chicken parts. Cover with foil or a tight-fitting lid and bake in a 350° F. oven for 45 minutes, or until tender. Uncover the baking dish the last 10 minutes so chicken will brown.

Makes 8 servings.

Broiled Chicken Rosemary

SENSITIVITY CHECKLIST:

This recipe is   **dairy** _____-free

egg ✓-free

wheat ✓-free

corn ✓-free

sugar ✓-free

This is a fast delicious way to make broiled chicken when you're in a hurry. The bit of rosemary herb gives it a delightful flavor.

2 small split broiler chickens, about 2 pounds each
2 tablespoons melted butter
2 tablespoons lemon juice
¼ teaspoon salt
⅛ teaspoon pepper
¼ teaspoon rosemary

Place halves of chicken on a broiling pan, skin side down. Combine butter, lemon juice, salt, pepper, and rosemary, stirring well. Brush half of this mixture on top of chicken and broil for 10 minutes. Turn chicken, brush the skin side with the remaining mixture and broil for 10 minutes more, or until tender.

Makes 4 servings.

Chicken Stew

SENSITIVITY CHECKLIST:

This recipe is

✔-free

dairy

✔-free

egg

✔-free

wheat

____-free

corn

✔-free

sugar

If child is on a corn-free regime, substitute wheat flour for cornstarch in this recipe.

2 chicken fryers, cut up
2 teaspoons salt
1 bay leaf
¼ teaspoon thyme
5 cups water
2 cups celery, cut in 3-inch strips
2 cups carrots, cut in 3-inch strips
12 small white onions
⅓ cup cornstarch
1 cup water

Place chicken pieces, salt, bay leaf, thyme, and water in a large kettle. Bring to a boil, reduce heat, and simmer, covered, 30 minutes. Add celery, carrots, and onions. Simmer, covered, about 10 minutes or until vegetables are tender. Mix cornstarch and 1 cup water; stir into chicken mixture. Bring to a boil; stirring constantly, and boil 1 minute. Serve in soup plates.

Makes 8 servings.

Baked Crusted Chicken

SENSITIVITY CHECKLIST:

This recipe is  _____-free

dairy

_____-free

egg

_____-free

wheat

_____-free

corn

_____-free

sugar

Check label of peanut butter to be sure that it is pure. Otherwise purchase at a health food store or make it yourself. If the child has been placed on a corn-free diet use another vegetable oil or dot with butter.

1 egg, slightly beaten
⅓ cup creamy or chunk-style peanut butter
1 teaspoon salt
⅛ teaspoon pepper
⅓ cup milk
8 chicken drumsticks
1 cup fine dry bread crumbs (see Index)
¼ cup corn oil

Mix together egg, peanut butter, salt, and pepper. Gradually add milk, beating with a fork to blend. Dip chicken in egg mixture; then in crumbs. Place in an oiled 13-by-9-by-2-inch baking pan. Sprinkle remaining corn oil over chicken pieces. Bake in a 375° F. oven 45 minutes or until chicken is tender.

Makes 4 servings.

Roast Chicken

Just a little extra seasoning seems to make all the difference between a good chicken and one that tastes great. This same method may be used for a pair of small fryers that you plan to roast.

1 roasting chicken, about 5 pounds
1 lemon
1 teaspoon salt
½ teaspoon paprika
2 sprigs parsley
1 small onion, sliced
1 cup water

Arrange roasting chicken in an open pan, after cleaning and washing thoroughly. Cut lemon in half and squeeze the juice over the surfaces of the chicken, including the interior. Sprinkle salt both inside and outside. Sprinkle the skin with paprika. Tuck remaining squeezed-out lemon halves and parsley into the chicken. Place onion slices around the base of the chicken and pour water into the pan. Roast in a 350° F. oven about 2½ hours, basting occasionally with pan juices. Remove lemon rinds and parsley from chicken cavity before serving.

Makes 4 to 6 servings.

Stuffed Roast Chicken

SENSITIVITY CHECKLIST:

This recipe is dairy ___✓___-free

egg ___✓___-free

wheat _____-free

corn ___✓___-free

sugar ___✓___-free

Never stuff the bird in advance, although you may prepare the stuffing and refrigerate it until ready to stuff and cook the chicken. The cold of the refrigerator is not sufficient to reach the interior of the bird and will not prevent potentially dangerous bacterial growth. For the same reason, always remove leftover stuffing from the roasted bird and refrigerate separately.

1 roasting chicken, 4 to 5 pounds
1 teaspoon salt
2 cups soft bread crumbs (see Index)
2 tablespoons chopped parsley
2 tablespoons chopped celery leaves
2 tablespoons chopped onion
¼ teaspoon thyme
¼ cup water
¼ teaspoon paprika

Wash chicken and pat dry. Sprinkle with salt, inside and outside. Combine bread crumbs, parsley, celery leaves, onion, and thyme. Add water. Spoon stuffing into chicken cavity, being careful not to pack it too tightly. Sprinkle paprika over chicken. Place chicken on a rack in a roasting pan and roast in a preheated 325° F. oven for about 2½ hours or until tender.

Makes 6 servings.

Orange-roasted Chicken

SENSITIVITY CHECKLIST:

This recipe is ____-free *dairy*

✓ -free *egg*

✓ -free *wheat*

____-free *corn*

____-free *sugar*

Brown sugar may be omitted if the child has been placed on a sugar-free regime. If child has been placed on a natural salicylate-free diet, omit this recipe until permission has been granted to resume the use of oranges.

1 roasting chicken, about 5 pounds
4 tablespoons butter, melted
1 teaspoon salt
¼ teaspoon pepper
½ teaspoon dried rosemary leaves
2 small oranges, cut in half
¼ cup cornstarch
2 cups orange juice
1 cup chicken stock (see Index)
1 tablespoon brown sugar

Place chicken in roasting pan. Brush with butter. Season with salt, pepper, and rosemary. Place oranges in cavity of chicken. Tie legs. Bake in a 325° F. oven, basting occasionally, about 2½ hours or until skin is browned and leg joint moves easily. Remove chicken to platter. Measure fat drippings and return ¼ cup to roasting pan. Sprinkle cornstarch into pan drippings. Stir and cook over medium heat just until smooth; remove from heat. Gradually stir in orange juice, chicken stock, and sugar until smooth. Bring to a boil over medium heat, stirring constantly, and boil 2 minutes. Serve gravy over chicken.

Makes about 6 servings.

Chicken Almond Salad

SENSITIVITY CHECKLIST:

This recipe is  ___✓___-free

___-free

___✓___-free

___✓___-free

___✓___-free

Deliberately cook too much chicken for dinner and use it for salad the next day. Prepare salad, refrigerate, and serve on lettuce or use as a spread on bread. If the child is placed on a natural salicylate-free diet, omit almonds from this recipe until permission has been granted to resume the use of almonds.

1½ cups finely chopped cooked chicken
3 tablespoons slivered blanched almonds
¼ cup diced celery
2 tablespoons grated carrot
½ cup mayonnaise (see Index)
¼ teaspoon salt
Dash of pepper

Combine all ingredients and use as salad or as a sandwich spread.

Makes 2½ cups.

NOTE: If the child is sensitive to corn oil use other salad oil in the preparation of the mayonnaise.

Creamy Chicken and Mushrooms

SENSITIVITY CHECKLIST:

This recipe is   _____-free
dairy

                   ✔-free
egg

                   ✔-free
wheat

                   _____-free
corn

                   ✔-free
sugar

No need to cook with the all-American condensed mushroom soup trick when you have a recipe like this to follow. Add peas for extra color and nutrition.

6 tablespoons butter
8 ounces mushrooms, sliced
3 tablespoons cornstarch
1 teaspoon salt
¼ teaspoon pepper
½ teaspoon onion salt
3 cups milk
2 cups cooked diced chicken or turkey

In medium saucepan melt 2 tablespoons of butter. Add mushrooms and cook over medium heat about 3 minutes or until tender. Remove mushrooms, reserving pan juices. Heat remaining butter with juices in saucepan. Remove from heat. Add cornstarch, salt, pepper, and onion salt, stirring until smooth. Gradually add milk. Cook over medium heat, stirring constantly, until mixture comes to a boil and boils 1 minute. Stir in chicken and mushrooms until well mixed.

Makes 6 servings.

Chicken Livers and Mushrooms

SENSITIVITY CHECKLIST:

This recipe is  ✔-free *dairy*

✔-free *egg*

✔-free *wheat*

✔-free *corn*

✔-free *sugar*

This dish is great when served on rice, toast points, or freshly mashed potatoes. Good when you need to prepare a fast and filling supper.

½ cup chicken broth (see Index)
2 onions, thinly sliced
1½ pounds chicken livers
½ pound fresh mushrooms, sliced
2 tablespoons minced parsley
1 teaspoon paprika
½ teaspoon salt
⅛ teaspoon pepper

Pour chicken broth into a large skillet. Heat and add sliced onions; cook until translucent. Add chicken livers and mushrooms; sprinkle with parsley, paprika, salt, and pepper. Cover and simmer for 10 minutes, or until livers are tender.

Makes 4 servings.

Rock Cornish Hens

SENSITIVITY CHECKLIST:

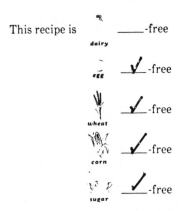

This recipe is   ____-free
dairy

✓-free
egg

✓-free
wheat

✓-free
corn

✓-free
sugar

These tiny hens are often a good buy at the food market in frozen form. For best results, thaw in the refrigerator for a day before cooking.

3 Rock Cornish hens, 1½ pounds each
1 lemon
¾ teaspoon salt
¼ teaspoon pepper
3 tablespoons melted butter
Paprika

Rinse and dry hens. (Each hen should serve 2; if hens are under 1 pound each, prepare one for each person.) Rub inside and outside with lemon cut in half. Cut up lemon and tuck pieces into cavity of the hens. Season hens with salt and pepper. Brush with melted butter and dust lightly with paprika. Roast in a 350° F. oven for 45 minutes to 1 hour, depending on size. Serve at once.

Makes 6 servings.

Roast Turkey with Orange Glaze

SENSITIVITY CHECKLIST:

This recipe is  ____-free

                ✔-free

                ✔-free

                ✔-free

                ✔-free

If child has been placed on a natural salicylate-free diet, omit the orange juice and increase the amount of butter to baste turkey. For a treat, use leftovers in the recipe for Turkey Tetrazzini (recipe follows).

1 large roasting turkey
1 teaspoon salt
1 teaspoon paprika
¼ cup butter
½ cup orange juice

Thaw turkey, clean, and season with salt and paprika. Melt butter in a small saucepan; stir in orange juice. Use about a fourth of this mixture to brush all over the skin of the turkey. Place turkey on a rack in a large roasting pan. Roast in a 325° F. oven for approximately 20 minutes to the pound, uncovered for the first hour and then loosely tented with aluminum foil for the remaining cooking time. Baste turkey every half hour with the remaining butter sauce. To test for doneness, jiggle the drumstick. It will move easily when the bird is thoroughly cooked. Or use a meat thermometer inserted deep into the thickest part of the white meat, near the thigh. When it reaches a temperature of 190° F. the bird is done. To make gravy, remove the bird from the pan and pour in a small amount of boiling water, scraping in the drippings that have stuck to the pan. Set pan over medium heat and bring to a simmer, stirring until you have as much gravy as you require. The turkey will benefit from the "rest" while you are preparing the gravy—it will be easier to carve about 20 minutes after being removed from the oven.

———

NOTE: If you intend to freeze turkey slices, thin the remaining gravy with water and submerge slices in it. The turkey slices will be more moist when reheated.

Turkey Tetrazzini

SENSITIVITY CHECKLIST:

This recipe is ____-free *dairy*

____✓-free *egg*

____-free *wheat*

____✓-free *corn*

____✓-free *sugar*

Use the turkey carcass to make broth. Then prepare casserole for the next day, or freeze after baking and use within two months. To reheat, place frozen casserole in a cold oven set at 350° F. and bake for 45 minutes.

8 ounces spaghetti (no artificial additives)
3 cups diced cooked turkey
6 tablespoons butter
½ pound fresh mushrooms, sliced
1 tablespoon lemon juice
3 tablespoons flour
2 cups turkey or chicken broth (see Index)
1 cup heavy cream
½ teaspoon salt
⅛ teaspoon pepper
⅛ teaspoon nutmeg
½ cup grated Parmesan cheese

Cook spaghetti as directed on the package; drain and rinse to prevent the spaghetti from getting sticky. Place spaghetti in a greased casserole; toss with turkey. Melt butter in a large skillet and sauté mushrooms; sprinkle with lemon juice. Stir in flour until mixture thickens, then slowly stir in broth. As the mixture begins to thicken and bubble, stir in heavy cream, salt, pepper, and nutmeg. Finally stir in half of the cheese. Stir constantly as the mixture thickens; then pour over the spaghetti and mix thoroughly. Top with the remaining cheese and bake in a pre-heated 350° F. oven for 30 minutes.

Makes 6 servings.

9

Fish

More people are beginning to learn what fish lovers have always known—fish is an easily digestible, high protein, low fat food. When the hyperactive child is placed on a rotation diet, you'll want to learn how to prepare some new fish dishes to vary the offerings.

If you're buying a whole fish and are concerned about freshness, look at the eyes. They should be bright, clear, and slightly bulging. Press the skin if you can; if the pressure leaves no mark of indentation, the fish is fresh. Look at the gills to see that they are bright red. Sniff a bit too; there should be only a fresh sea odor. Refrigerate fish immediately and use it within a day for best results.

There may be a time when some fisherman gives you too many whole fish to use at once. Clean them, wash, and pat dry. Flash freeze them on a flat tray for several hours and then remove the fish one at a time to dip immediately into icy water. This will form a thin coating of ice on the fish. Wrap in foil without breaking the ice coating, and freeze at once. This technique will enable you to keep those fish for many months.

You'll need one-third to one-half pound per person of dressed fish, and one pound per person of whole fish that has to be trimmed of its scales, entrails, head, fins and tail. The first rule when cooking fish is to be gentle with it: don't overcook it; poach it rather than boil it; and be prepared to serve it as soon as it is ready.

In case you're new at cooking most kinds of fish, here's some information that you may find to be helpful:

HOW TO BAKE: Place steaks, fillets, or whole fish in a greased baking dish. Brush with seasoned butter, and bake in a preheated oven at approximately 350° F. or at the temperature suggested in the recipe. Stuff whole fish with an herb and bread stuffing, or marinate fish before baking. For frozen fish, follow package directions.

HOW TO BROIL: Arrange steaks, fillets, or whole fish on a preheated, well-greased broiler rack. Brush with melted butter or basting sauce. For steaks and fillets, place rack about 2 inches from heat; for whole or split fish, place rack 3 to 6 inches from heat. Fillets and split fish do not need to be turned. Turn steaks and whole fish once, basting again, to broil second side. Serve immediately.

HOW TO PAN-FRY: This method is usually reserved for small whole fish such as trout. Other forms such as fillets, steaks, and drawn fish may be pan-fried although broiling is generally preferred. Bread the fish by dipping first in milk, then into bread crumbs. Use melted shortening or vegetable oil to cover bottom of pan, about ⅛ inch deep. Fry fish until light brown, turn, and brown other side. Too high temperature will cause fat to smoke. Serve on a hot platter.

HOW TO OVEN FRY: This is the method most often used to cook frozen breaded fillets, sticks, or portions. (Read labels to be sure ingredients are all natural.) Place the breaded fish in a shallow, lightly greased pan or on a baking sheet and bake according to package directions.

HOW TO DEEP-FRY: Use a deep, heavy, 3-quart saucepan and fill halfway with oil or melted vegetable shortening. Heat slowly until 375° F., using a thermometer to check temperature. Frying at too low a temperature causes foods to soak up shortening; at too high a temperature, shortening will smoke and cause disagreeable odors and flavors. Place fish in the bottom of the fryer basket or on a large slotted spoon and lower into pan. Fry until golden brown; drain and serve immediately. Allow shortening to return to 375° F. before adding a second batch.

HOW TO POACH: Place fish on a flat, greased tray of a poacher, on a strip of greased heavy-duty foil, or in cheesecloth. Lower into the poacher or saucepan and cover with seasoned liquid. Simmer gently until fish is cooked and then remove from liquid. The liquid in which the fish is poached might be a fish stock, court bouillon, or wine (if child is not on a natural salicylate-free diet) that may be used as a base for a sauce for the fish.

HOW TO STEAM: Steaming is much like poaching, except that the fish is placed over the liquid rather than into it. Place fish in a deep pan on a greased perforated rack or tray that will hold it above liquid level. Bring liquid to a boil and cover pan tightly. Cook until done. Season and salt fish after steaming. Liquid used in steaming can be the base for sauce for the fish.

The following recipes will give you some good fish dishes to start you on your way. The one reward will be that fish cooks quickly. If you buy fresh fish, it can't help but taste flavorful.

Sole Rolls

SENSITIVITY CHECKLIST:

This recipe is   dairy   _____-free

egg   ✓-free

wheat   ✓-free

corn   ✓-free

sugar   ✓-free

Be sure to check the label on the package of chive cream cheese to be certain that no artificial additives are listed. Use extra paprika if a more colorful appearance is desired.

4 fillets of sole
1 package (3 ounces) chive cream cheese
2 tablespoons milk
½ teaspoon salt
⅛ teaspoon pepper
⅛ teaspoon paprika
¼ cup light cream

Spread one side of sole slices with chive cream cheese softened with milk. Roll up. Place in buttered baking dish. Sprinkle with salt, pepper, and paprika. Pour cream around fish. Bake in a 375° F. oven for 20 minutes.

Makes 4 servings.

Cashew Banana Sole

SENSITIVITY CHECKLIST:

This recipe is  _____-free
dairy

___✓_-free
egg

___✓_-free
wheat

___✓_-free
corn

___✓_-free
sugar

If you prefer to broil the fish, slip it under the broiler, uncovered, for about 10 minutes, or until fish flakes easily. Then cover with sauce as directed below and serve at once.

4 large fillets of sole
½ teaspoon salt
⅛ teaspoon pepper
4 tablespoons butter
·2 bananas, sliced
2 tablespoons lemon juice
¼ cup chopped cashew nuts

Arrange fish fillets flat in a buttered baking dish. Sprinkle with salt and pepper. Dot with 3 tablespoons of the butter. Cover tightly and bake in a 350° F. oven for 20 minutes. Meanwhile, toss banana slices with lemon juice. Melt remaining 1 tablespoon butter in a skillet. Add cashews and sliced banana; cook over low heat for several minutes. Spoon over cooked fish.

Makes 4 servings.

Mushroom-sauced Flounder

SENSITIVITY CHECKLIST:

This recipe is ⬚ ____-free

dairy

○ ✓-free

egg

✓-free

wheat

✓-free

corn

✓-free

sugar

This is a good recipe to choose when you want to cook a fast but delicious dinner. Prepare your vegetables first, as the fish is best served when cooked. Who really needs convenience foods for speed in the kitchen?

4 slices fillet of flounder
½ cup lemon juice
¼ teaspoon salt
⅛ teaspoon pepper
3 tablespoons butter
¼ pound fresh mushrooms, sliced
¼ teaspoon dried dill

Arrange fillets of flounder in one layer in a flat baking dish. Pour lemon juice over and refrigerate, covered, for at least 1 hour. When ready to broil, sprinkle with the salt and pepper and slip under the broiler for about 10 minutes, or until fish flakes easily. (Don't worry about the excess lemon juice in the pan, it will evaporate.) Meanwhile, melt butter in a skillet and sauté mushrooms for several minutes until golden and limp. Add dill. Spoon over broiled fish and serve at once.

Makes 4 servings.

Flounder Florentine

This recipe is ____-free

_____✓_-free

_____✓_-free

_____✓_-free

_____✓_-free

For variety, add some grated Parmesan cheese to the spinach mixture. Another time add some tiny pignola nuts—a few tablespoons go a long way.

4 slices fillet of flounder
1 package (10 ounces) frozen chopped spinach, thawed
1 tablespoon grated onion
¼ teaspoon nutmeg
¼ teaspoon salt
2 tablespoons melted butter
2 tablespoons lemon juice
Paprika

Spread fillets of flounder flat. Combine spinach, onion, nutmeg, and salt; spread in a thin layer over top surface of fillets. Roll up and fasten with toothpicks if necessary. Place in a greased baking pan. Combine melted butter and lemon juice; brush over tops of fish rolls. Sprinkle with paprika. Bake uncovered in a 350° F. oven for 10 minutes, or until fish flakes easily.

Makes 4 servings.

Fish Parmigiana

SENSITIVITY CHECKLIST:

This recipe is ____-free (dairy)

✓_-free (egg)

✓_-free (wheat)

✓_-free (corn)

✓_-free (sugar)

For best results, grate the Parmesan cheese freshly just before using. It has a much better flavor than the packaged variety of grated cheese. Add extra oregano if everyone likes it.

1 pound fillets of flounder
2 tablespoons lemon juice
½ teaspoon salt
⅛ teaspoon pepper
1 tablespoon grated onion
½ teaspoon oregano
2 tablespoons grated Parmesan cheese
1 tablespoon butter

Arrange flounder fillets on a broiling pan. Sprinkle with lemon juice. Season with salt and pepper. Add grated onion, oregano, and then grated cheese. Dot with butter. Broil for 10 to 15 minutes, or until fish flakes easily.

Makes 4 servings.

Halibut au Gratin

SENSITIVITY CHECKLIST:

This recipe is   ____-free   *dairy*

✓-free   *egg*

____-free   *wheat*

✓-free   *corn*

✓-free   *sugar*

Be sure to have several colorful vegetables to add eye appeal when you serve bland-looking fish. Taste buds start stirring when the platter is attractive.

1 onion
½ pound fresh mushrooms
2 tablespoons minced parsley
4 halibut steaks
¼ cup lemon juice
½ teaspoon salt
⅛ teaspoon pepper
½ cup light cream
¼ cup fine bread crumbs (see Index)
2 tablespoons grated hard white cheese
4 teaspoons butter
4 lemon wedges

Chop onion and mushrooms, and mix together with parsley. Place in a thin layer over bottom of a buttered baking dish. Arrange fish on top. Sprinkle with lemon juice, salt, and pepper. Pour cream around fish. Sprinkle bread crumbs and cheese over fish and dot with butter. Bake in a 375° F. oven for 30 minutes. Serve with lemon wedges.

Makes 4 servings.

Broiled Halibut

This recipe is   _____-free
dairy

✓-free
egg

✓-free
wheat

✓-free
corn

✓-free
sugar

The thin coating of sour cream in this recipe creates a very special taste and texture. This is a good recipe to use when you have to cook dinner in a hurry.

1½ pounds halibut fillets
2 tablespoons lemon juice
¼ teaspoon salt
¼ teaspoon dill
½ cup dairy sour cream
½ teaspoon paprika

Arrange fillets in a single layer in a broiling pan. Sprinkle with lemon juice, salt, and dill. Spread a thin coating of sour cream over the top of each piece of fish. Sprinkle with paprika. Broil for about 15 minutes. The fish is cooked through if it flakes easily when touched with a fork.

Makes 4 servings.

Fish Salad

SENSITIVITY CHECKLIST:

This recipe is

dairy　✓-free

egg　_____-free

wheat　✓-free

corn　✓-free

sugar　✓-free

Deliberately plan to cook too much fish for dinner. Flake the excess for this salad. Prepare the salad after dinner. Cover and refrigerate to use for salad or as a sandwich spread next day.

1 pound flounder or halibut, cooked and flaked
2 tablespoons lemon juice
½ cup chopped celery
¼ teaspoon salt
¼ teaspoon dill
½ cup mayonnaise (see Index)

Mix flaked fish, lemon juice, celery, salt, and dill. Add mayonnaise. Makes 2½ cups.

NOTE: If the child is sensitive to corn oil, use other salad oil in preparing mayonnaise.

Stuffed Bluefish

This recipe is _____-free

✔-free

_____-free

✔-free

✔-free

This stuffing may be used for any whole fish that you plan to bake. If possible, have your fishman remove the bone structure.

1 whole bluefish, about 4 pounds, cleaned
2 tablespoons butter
1 small onion, diced
1 cup bread crumbs (see Index)
½ cup chopped celery
1 teaspoon finely chopped parsley
½ teaspoon salt
¼ cup milk
1 lemon

Melt butter in a skillet; sauté onion until tender. Stir in bread crumbs; add celery, parsley, and salt. Stir in milk. Wash and wipe bluefish; stuff with prepared mixture. Cut lemon in half and squeeze over fish. Place fish in a greased pan. Bake for 15 minutes per pound of fish in a 375° F. oven.

Makes 4 servings.

Baked Red Snapper in Sauce

SENSITIVITY CHECKLIST:

This recipe is   _____-free
dairy

✔-free
egg

_____-free
wheat

✔-free
corn

✔-free
sugar

If child has been placed on a natural salicylate-free diet avoid the use of this recipe until permission has been granted to resume the use of tomatoes. Remove bay leaves just before serving.

1 red snapper, about 3 pounds, cleaned
⅓ cup flour
½ teaspoon salt
⅛ teaspoon pepper
3 tablespoons butter
1 small onion, diced
1 cup diced celery
1 small green pepper, diced
1 clove garlic, minced
4 tomatoes, skinned and chopped
½ teaspoon chili powder
¼ cup lemon juice
2 bay leaves

Lightly dredge fish in mixture of flour, salt, and pepper. Place in a buttered baking dish. Melt butter in a skillet; sauté onion, celery, green pepper, and garlic until all are limp. Add chopped tomatoes, chili powder, and lemon juice. Pour this mixture around the fish. Add bay leaves. Bake uncovered in a 350° F. oven for 45 minutes, or until fish flakes easily. Baste occasionally with sauce.

Makes 4 to 6 servings.

Boiled Salmon with Dill Sauce

SENSITIVITY CHECKLIST:

This recipe is _____-free (dairy)

✓-free (egg)

✓-free (wheat)

✓-free (corn)

✓-free (sugar)

This salmon is tasty whether it is served hot or cold. If you like the flavor of dill, add a sprig to the boiling water when cooking the fish.

4 small salmon steaks
Boiling water
1 lemon, thinly sliced
1 teaspoon salt
1 cup plain yogurt
2 tablespoons chopped chives
1 tablespoon lemon juice
1 tablespoon minced fresh dill

Place salmon steaks on a rack in the bottom of a fish poacher or large skillet. Cover with boiling water. Add sliced lemon and ½ teaspoon salt. Simmer for about 10 minutes, or until fish flakes easily but holds its shape. Remove fish and serve hot or cold with Dill Sauce.

To prepare Dill Sauce, empty yogurt into a bowl. Stir in chives. Add lemon juice, ½ teaspoon salt, and dill.

Makes 4 servings.

Salmon Croquettes

This recipe is ✓-free (dairy)

_____-free (egg)

_____-free (wheat)

✓-free (corn)

✓-free (sugar)

Prepare the salmon mixture the night before. Cover and refrigerate until ready to shape and cook the croquettes for dinner. Serve the child's portion with homemade mayonnaise, if the rest of the family is using prepared tartar sauce.

1 can (16 ounces) salmon, drained and flaked
½ cup soft bread crumbs (see Index)
½ cup mayonnaise (see Index)
2 eggs, beaten
2 tablespoons diced green pepper
1 tablespoon grated onion
½ teaspoon salt
¼ teaspoon paprika
¼ teaspoon dry mustard
1 teaspoon lemon juice
Additional soft bread crumbs
¼ cup cooking oil

Combine salmon, the ½ cup bread crumbs, mayonnaise, eggs, green pepper, onion, salt, paprika, mustard, and lemon juice. Chill mixture for several hours. Shape salmon mixture into 12 small or 8 large croquettes. Coat with the additional bread crumbs until well covered. Heat oil in a large skillet over medium heat; brown croquettes on all sides. Drain on paper towels.

Makes 4 servings.

NOTE: If the child is sensitive to corn oil, use other salad oil in preparing mayonnaise.

Broiled Scampi

SENSITIVITY CHECKLIST:

This recipe is ⎰ ✓-free
dairy

 ✓-free
egg

 ✓-free
wheat

 ✓-free
corn

 ____-free
sugar

For variety, add oregano to this recipe. If the child is on a completely sugar-free diet, omit the sugar. Excellent when served on a bed of hot cooked rice.

1 pound large shrimp, peeled and cleaned, with tails on
2 tablespoons olive oil
1 clove crushed garlic
1 tablespoon minced fresh parsley
½ teaspoon brown sugar
½ teaspoon salt
¼ teaspoon pepper
Lemon wedges

Split the shrimp into a butterfly shape, leaving tails on. Combine oil, garlic, parsley, brown sugar, salt, and pepper. Arrange shrimp on a broiling pan, brush with oil mixture and broil for 3 minutes on each side. Serve with lemon wedges.

Makes 4 servings.

Shrimp Oriental

SENSITIVITY CHECKLIST:

This recipe is
dairy ✓-free

egg ✓-free

wheat ✓-free

corn ____-free

sugar ✓-free

Here's a good wheat-free recipe to use when cooking delectable shrimp. If the child is sensitive to corn, use flour in place of cornstarch and another kind of oil in place of corn oil.

1½ teaspoons cornstarch
½ teaspoon salt
⅛ teaspoon ginger
1 tablespoon lemon juice
1 pound shrimp, shelled and deveined
2 tablespoons corn oil
1 scallion, chopped

Combine cornstarch, salt, and ginger. Stir in lemon juice. Toss with shrimp, coating evenly. Heat corn oil in skillet. Add shrimp and sauté over medium-high heat 5 to 7 minutes, stirring occasionally. Add scallions.

Makes 4 servings.

Shrimp Fried Rice

SENSITIVITY CHECKLIST:

This recipe is

dairy ✓-free

egg ____-free

wheat ✓-free

corn ____-free

sugar ✓-free

When you need a way to stretch a pound of shrimp to serve six people, try this Oriental recipe. Be sure the rice is cooked first as the entire procedure is another quick-cooking experience. Serve with pure soy sauce, if desired.

1 pound shrimp, fresh or frozen, deveined, diced
2 tablespoons chopped green onion
1 teaspoon cornstarch
2½ teaspoons salt
¼ teaspoon pepper
¼ cup corn oil
3 cups cooked rice
2 eggs, slightly beaten

In a large bowl stir together shrimp, green onion, cornstarch, 1 teaspoon salt and pepper. In wok or skillet heat corn oil over medium-high heat. Add shrimp mixture. Cook, stirring constantly, 3 to 5 minutes or until shrimp turns pink. Remove from wok with slotted spoon. In medium bowl stir together cooked rice, eggs, and 1½ teaspoons salt. Place in wok. Cook, stirring constantly, over medium-high heat, about 2 minutes or until egg is cooked. Add shrimp mixture and cook, stirring constantly, until heated.

Makes 6 servings.

Fried Scallops

SENSITIVITY CHECKLIST:

This recipe is   _✓_-free

   dairy

   ____-free

   egg

   ____-free

   wheat

   _✓_-free

   corn

   _✓_-free

   sugar

Fine bread crumbs may be used in place of the soda cracker crumbs in this recipe. If child is sensitive to corn oil, use another kind for frying scallops.

1 pint (about 1 pound) fresh scallops
½ cup flour
1 cup mayonnaise (see Index)
1 cup soda cracker crumbs
1 cup cooking oil

Cut large scallops in half; if using bay scallops leave them whole. Roll in flour, dip in mayonnaise until evenly coated, then roll in crumbs. Pour oil into a skillet and heat until a 1-inch bread cube turns brown in 40 seconds. Fry scallops in hot oil until golden brown, about 3 minutes. Drain on paper toweling.

Makes 4 servings.

Scallop en Casserole

SENSITIVITY CHECKLIST:

This recipe is   dairy   ____-free

     egg   ✓-free

     wheat   ____-free

     corn   ____-free

     sugar   ✓-free

If child is sensitive to corn, change cornstarch to wheat flour in this recipe. It's the kind of recipe that you can prepare several hours before serving, refrigerate, and then place in oven to heat.

2 cups uncooked shell macaroni
1 pound fresh sea scallops or frozen scallops, thawed
4 tablespoons butter
1 clove garlic, crushed
3 tablespoons cornstarch
2 teaspoons salt
¼ teaspoon pepper
2¾ cups milk
2 cups shredded mild white Cheddar cheese

Cook macaroni according to package directions; drain. If scallops are large, cut in half. Melt butter in a 3-quart saucepan over low heat. Add garlic and sauté about 5 minutes. Add cornstarch, salt, and pepper; stir until well blended. Gradually add milk, stirring until mixture is smooth. Cook over medium heat, stirring constantly, until mixture thickens and boils 2 minutes. Stir in 1½ cups of the cheese. Mix together cornstarch mixture, scallops, and macaroni and place in a 2-quart casserole. Sprinkle remaining ½ cup cheese over top. Bake in a 350° F. oven 30 minutes or until thoroughly heated.

Makes 4 to 6 servings.

Scalloped Oysters

SENSITIVITY CHECKLIST:

This recipe is   _____-free   **dairy**

✓ -free   **egg**

_____-free   **wheat**

✓ -free   **corn**

✓ -free   **sugar**

If you've ever wondered how to cook oysters easily, here's a way that all will enjoy. Bread crumbs may be substituted for the crushed soda crackers, if desired.

1 quart shucked oysters, with liquor
2 cups coarsely crushed soda crackers
½ cup butter
1 tablespoon chopped parsley
½ teaspoon salt
⅛ teaspoon pepper
1 to 2 cups milk

In a greased 2-quart casserole, place alternate layers of oysters with liquor and crackers, dotting each layer with butter and sprinkling with parsley, salt, and pepper. End with layer of crumbs. Add milk until liquid almost reaches top of casserole. Dot with remaining butter. Bake in a 350° F. oven until browned, 45 to 60 minutes.

Makes 6 to 8 servings.

Crab Meat Bake

SENSITIVITY CHECKLIST:

This recipe is | dairy _____-free

egg _____-free

wheat _____-free

corn ✓-free

sugar ✓-free

Canned or frozen crab meat may be used for this dish. Add a layer of cooked chopped spinach underneath, if desired.

1 pound cooked crab meat
1 cup Seafood Herb Dressing (recipe follows)
2 tablespoons bread crumbs (see Index)
2 tablespoons butter

Combine crab meat with dressing in a buttered ovenproof pan. Sprinkle with bread crumbs and dot with butter. Broil for 5 minutes or until lightly browned and bubbly.

Seafood Herb Dressing

SENSITIVITY CHECKLIST:

This recipe is   _____-free
dairy

_____-free
egg

__✓__-free
wheat

__✓__-free
corn

__✓__-free
sugar

This dressing will keep for about a week if stored tightly covered in the refrigerator. It adds a very complementary flavor to most kinds of fish.

½ cup mayonnaise (see Index)
½ cup yogurt
1 tablespoon finely chopped parsley
1½ teaspoons chopped chives
1½ teaspoons dried tarragon leaves
½ teaspoon chopped dill

Mix together the mayonnaise and yogurt. Add the parsley, chives, tarragon, and dill. Chill at least 2 hours before serving.

Makes 1 cup dressing.

10

Vegetables

When you are seeking a variety of vegetables to add color and texture to a rotation diet, you will undoubtedly discover a few new ones that you are not accustomed to preparing. They will all help you to plan menus for four days without repetition. You'll find that your cooking will grow more interesting too.

There are only a few important rules to remember about vegetable cookery. Wash all fresh produce carefully before cooking and, to preserve their nutrients, cook in the least amount of liquid possible. Peel vegetables paper thin, so you don't throw away valuable minerals. And avoid reheating vegetables so they lose flavor and vitamins when cooked too long. It is a good idea to get in the habit of tossing refrigerated leftover vegetables with your salad greens for a change of pace there too.

If you wonder about whether to cover the pot or not, there's a good rule of thumb to follow: If it grows under the ground, cover it; if it grows above ground, don't.

To help you discover new kinds of vegetables to buy and serve, here is a list of marketing and storing tips to assist you in getting the most for your precious food dollars:

ASPARAGUS: Stalks should be mostly green with compact tips. Remove tough white parts of stalks. Store in refrigerator crisper in a plastic bag. Use within 1 or 2 days.

BEANS, LIMA: Select well-filled pods that are clean, fresh, and of good color. Old and tough beans will have shriveled, spotted, or flabby pods. Shelled lima beans should be plump and of good green or green-white color. Refrigerate and use within 1 or 2 days.

BEANS, SNAP: Select pods with small seeds, as overmature pods may be tough. Avoid dry-looking or wilted pods. Refrigerate and use within 1 or 2 days.

BEETS: Select smooth and firm beets. Soft or shriveled beets may be tough. Store beets, covered, in the refrigerator, and use within 1 or 2 weeks.

BROCCOLI: Select stalks that are clean with compact green clusters. Avoid those with yellow flower clusters. The stalks should be dark green, tender, and firm. Dirty spots may indicate insects. Store in refrigerator in a plastic bag and use within 1 or 2 days.

BRUSSELS SPROUTS: Select firm sprouts of good green color. Avoid those that have worm-eaten or wilted leaves, or a dirty appearance. Store in the refrigerator in a plastic bag and use within 1 or 2 days.

CABBAGE: Select crisp, firm heads that feel heavy for their size. Avoid those that are discolored, soft, or have wormholes. Store in plastic bag in the refrigerator and use within 1 or 2 weeks.

CARROTS: Select those of good color that are smooth and firm. Avoid wilted or shriveled carrots, large-sized ones that may have a pithy core, and those that are cracked. Remove tips and tops and store in a plastic bag in the refrigerator for 1 to 2 weeks.

CAULIFLOWER: Select a white, clean, firm, and compact head with fresh green leaves. Avoid spotted or bruised heads. Store, covered, in the refrigerator and use within 3 to 5 days.

CELERY: Select crisp, clean celery with branches that will snap easily. Avoid soft, pithy, or stringy stalks. Wrap in plastic bag and store in crisper in refrigerator. Use within 1 or 2 weeks.

CORN: Select ears with plump kernels and fresh green husks. Avoid dry or yellowed husks. Cook as soon after purchase as possible.

CUCUMBERS:　Select firm, green, well-shaped cucumbers. Avoid those that are withered or overmature, and those that have decay spots. Store in refrigerator crisper and use within 3 to 5 days.

EGGPLANT:　Select firm, dark purple, heavy eggplant. Avoid those that are soft and scarred. Decay appears as brown spots on the surface. Store in a cool place (60° F.) or store in refrigerator in a plastic bag. Use within 3 to 5 days.

LETTUCE:　Select crisp, clean heads that are firm and heavy for their size. Avoid those that have rust spots and those with an excess of outer leaves. Wash and dry before storing; wrap in paper toweling and store in crisper in refrigerator. Use within 1 to 2 days.

MUSHROOMS:　Select clean, white, firm mushrooms with light-colored gills on the underside. Avoid dark and discolored mushrooms. Store in a plastic bag in the refrigerator and use within 1 or 2 days.

ONIONS:　Select clean, hard onions with dry skins; avoid those with developing seed-stem and those that feel moist at the neck, which is an indication of decay inside. Store in a cool place (60° F.) and they will keep for a month or so.

PARSLEY:　Select bright-green, crisp-appearing leaves; avoid yellowing wilted-looking leaves. Wash thoroughly, shake dry, and place in a tightly covered jar in the refrigerator. Use within 1 or 2 weeks.

PEAS:　Select light-green, firm, and well-filled pods; avoid flat, wilted, or yellowing pods. Store in pods in refrigerator until wanted. Use within 1 or 2 days.

PEPPERS:　Select firm, fresh-colored peppers; avoid shriveled, spotted, or dull-appearing ones. Wash and dry. Store in crisper in the refrigerator and use within 3 to 5 days.

POTATOES:　Select firm, smooth, well-shaped potatoes; avoid sprouting, wilted, leathery, or discolored ones. Keep at room temperature and in a dark place for 3 to 4 weeks. When they are exposed to light, the exposed portion turns green and may taste bitter.

RADISHES: Select smooth, firm, crisp radishes of good color; avoid wilted, decayed, and pithy ones. Remove tops and store in a plastic bag in the crisper in the refrigerator. Use within 1 to 2 weeks.

SPINACH: Select leaves that are clean, crisp, and fresh-green in color; avoid wilted, bruised, and yellowed leaves. Decay appears as a slimy spot. Wash and dry. Wrap in paper toweling and store in the crisper of the refrigerator. Use within 1 or 2 days.

TOMATOES: Select well-formed plump and uniformly red ones; avoid those that have bruise marks or are soft or discolored. Store uncovered in the refrigerator crisper. Keep unripened tomatoes at room temperature away from direct sunlight until ripe, and then refrigerate. Use within 3 to 5 days.

ZUCCHINI: Select crisp, dark green zucchini; avoid soft spots, mold growth, and wilted appearance. Wash, dry, and wrap in plastic. Store in refrigerator. Use within 3 to 5 days.

As you can see, you should buy only the amount of vegetables that you will use within a short period of time, as they are highly perishable. Sort the vegetables before storing, and discard any that are bruised, soft, or decayed.

When purchasing frozen vegetables, avoid all products that have artificial additives. Do not buy any packages that are soft to the touch. It's wise to buy in a market that has a good turnover, and reach down in open cases for packages that are near the bottom of the freezer case. Do not buy packages that are piled above the safety line (look for it) in an open case, as they have been handled too much and are not in a position to remain safely frozen. Be sure that your own freezer is set at 0° F. and use an appropriate thermometer to test it. Otherwise your freezer will not be safe for longer than a few days' storage.

When purchasing canned vegetables, avoid those that have bulging ends, deep dents, or rust marks. If you open a can that has an off-odor or signs of mold, don't even taste the contents—just throw it out. Be sure to read every label to certify that only salt—not any of the sodiums listed with the artificial additives in chapter 2—has been added.

The recipes in this chapter are designed to show you how to make vegetables take their proper role in basic good nutrition. When the family has had a solid well-balanced meal there is less demand for sweets afterwards. And that's a help when trying to keep the hyperactive child on a limited carbohydrate regime.

Zesty Green Beans

SENSITIVITY CHECKLIST:

This recipe is  ✔-free

✔-free

✔-free

✔-free

✔-free

The following recipe can be cooked and chilled to serve as a cold side dish. Either way, it is a good change of pace when offering green beans.

1 package (10 ounces) frozen green beans
½ cup water
2 tablespoons white vinegar
½ teaspoon salt
⅛ teaspoon pepper
¼ teaspoon dry mustard
¼ teaspoon paprika

Place green beans in a saucepan. Combine water, vinegar, salt, pepper, mustard, and paprika in a glass; pour over the beans. Simmer until hot.

Makes 4 servings.

Green Beans and Mushrooms

SENSITIVITY CHECKLIST:

This recipe is   _____-free (dairy)

✔-free (egg)

✔-free (wheat)

✔-free (corn)

✔-free (sugar)

Here's a way to make the same old green beans a new and interesting taste treat. Make certain that the soy sauce is natural and pure.

2 packages (10 ounces each) frozen cut green beans
½ cup fresh sliced mushrooms
2 tablespoons butter
½ teaspoon pure soy sauce

Cook frozen green beans as directed on the package. Drain. Sauté mushrooms in butter; add green beans. Add soy sauce and toss lightly.

Makes 6 servings.

Orange-glazed Beets

SENSITIVITY CHECKLIST:

This recipe is   ____-free   *dairy*

   ✓-free   *egg*

   ____-free   *wheat*

   ✓-free   *corn*

   ✓-free   *sugar*

Honey is used as the sweetening agent in this recipe—if not allowed, omit. If child has been placed on a natural salicylate-free diet, omit this recipe until permission has been granted to resume the use of oranges.

1 can (1 pound) whole beets
1 tablespoon butter
2 teaspoons flour
1 teaspoon honey
½ cup orange juice

Heat beets in own liquid. Melt butter in a small saucepan; stir in flour until smooth. Remove from heat. Add honey and orange juice; stir until smooth. Return to heat, stirring constantly, until thickened. Drain hot beets; pour sauce over and serve.

Makes 4 servings.

Broccoli with Cheese Sauce

SENSITIVITY CHECKLIST:

This recipe is   ____-free
dairy

✓-free.
egg

____-free
wheat

✓-free
corn

✓-free
sugar

If dairy products are eliminated from the diet, prepare broccoli as directed below, omitting milk and cheese, and instead toss with slivered almonds heated in a tablespoon of olive oil.

4 heavy stalks fresh broccoli
¾ teaspoon salt
2 cups water
2 tablespoons butter
2 tablespoons flour
⅛ teaspoon pepper
1 cup milk
½ cup diced Swiss cheese

Wash broccoli stalks well. With a vegetable parer, scrape off the outer layer on the stalks (this will produce more tender broccoli in less cooking time). Cut each stalk lengthwise into quarters. Place in a saucepan with water and ½ teaspoon salt; cook broccoli about 12 minutes or until tender. Meanwhile, melt butter in a saucepan; blend in flour, ¼ teaspoon salt, and pepper. Stir constantly until smooth; then gradually stir in milk. Cook and stir until mixture boils; add cheese and stir until melted. Remove broccoli from water and drain; serve with cheese sauce.

Makes 4 servings.

Brussels Sprouts

SENSITIVITY CHECKLIST:

This recipe is  ____-free

____✔-free

____✔-free

____✔-free

____✔-free

It's amazing what a few pinches of herbs can do to a vegetable. Butter may be omitted if child is on a dairy-free regime.

1 package (10 ounces) frozen Brussels sprouts
1 cup water
1 teaspoon chopped parsley
½ teaspoon salt
¼ teaspoon dried marjoram
⅛ teaspoon white pepper
1 tablespoon butter

Cut Brussels sprouts in half lengthwise and place in a saucepan with water, parsley, salt, marjoram, and pepper. Cook for 5 minutes or until tender but not mushy. Drain. Toss lightly with butter and serve.

Makes 4 servings.

Glazed Carrots

SENSITIVITY CHECKLIST:

This recipe is ⬜ _____-free

dairy

○ ✓-free
egg

✓-free
wheat

✓-free
corn

✓-free
sugar

If child has been placed on a natural salicylate-free diet, eliminate orange juice in this recipe and substitute pineapple juice (no additives). Frozen cooked carrots or carrots canned in natural liquid may also be substituted if desired. Check whether small amounts of honey are permitted on the child's sugar-free diet, otherwise omit from recipe.

1 pound slender fresh carrots
2 tablespoons butter
1 tablespoon honey
½ cup orange juice
½ teaspoon salt
¼ teaspoon ginger

Scrape carrots and cut into ¼-inch diagonal slices. Cook in a small amount of water, covered, 15 to 20 minutes or until tender. Meanwhile, melt butter in a skillet; stir in honey and orange juice. Simmer 5 minutes. Stir in salt and ginger. Add cooked carrots, stirring carefully until they are completely glazed.

Makes 6 servings.

Carrots Tarragon

This recipe is  _____-free

dairy

✓-free

egg

✓-free

wheat

✓-free

corn

✓-free

sugar

Carrots may be scraped and sliced well ahead of time. Store them in a plastic bag in the refrigerator until ready to proceed with the recipe later in the day. Frozen cooked carrots or carrots canned in natural liquid may also be substituted if desired.

1 pound slender fresh carrots
1 cup water
1 teaspoon dried leaf tarragon
½ teaspoon salt
2 tablespoons butter

Scrape carrots and cut into ¼-inch crosswise slices. Place in a saucepan with water, tarragon, and salt. Cover and cook over medium heat about 20 minutes or until tender. Drain, add butter, and toss.

Makes 6 servings.

Creamed Cabbage with Walnuts

SENSITIVITY CHECKLIST:

This recipe is   _____-free   *dairy*

_____-free   *egg*

_____-free   *wheat*

_____-free   *corn*

✓-free   *sugar*

Recipe can be made corn-free by substituting wheat flour for cornstarch if child is sensitive to corn. It can be made wheat-free by omitting bread crumbs as a topping and following the recipe as written. Either way, it's a tasty way to prepare cabbage.

1 medium head cabbage, shredded
2 teaspoons salt
4 tablespoons butter
2 tablespoons cornstarch
¼ teaspoon pepper
2 cups milk
½ cup chopped walnuts
1 cup shredded hard white cheese
2 tablespoons fine dry bread crumbs (see Index)

Cook cabbage in 1-quart boiling water with 1 teaspoon salt, 7 minutes. Meanwhile, melt butter in a saucepan over medium heat. Remove from heat. Blend in cornstarch, 1 teaspoon salt and pepper. Gradually blend in milk. Cook over medium heat, stirring constantly, until mixture thickens and comes to boil. Drain cabbage well. Arrange alternate layers of cabbage, walnuts, sauce, and cheese in greased 1½-quart casserole, ending with layer of cheese. Sprinkle with bread crumbs. Bake in a 450° F. oven until heated and crumbs are lightly browned, about 10 minutes.

Makes 6 servings.

Baked Whole Cauliflower

SENSITIVITY CHECKLIST:

This recipe is  ____-free

_____-free

✓-free

_____-free

✓-free

✓-free

For a change of pace, just boil the cauliflower and serve with the Peanut Butter Vegetable Sauce at the end of this chapter. Children will clamor for more!

1 head of cauliflower, washed and trimmed
Water
¾ teaspoon salt
2 tablespoons butter
2 tablespoons flour
1 cup milk
⅛ teaspoon pepper
3 tablespoons fine bread crumbs (see Index)
1 tablespoon grated Parmesan cheese

Place cauliflower into a deep saucepan, cover with water, and add ½ teaspoon salt. Boil for 20 minutes, or until tender but not falling apart. Drain. Place whole in a buttered baking dish. Melt butter in a saucepan and add flour, stirring constantly until blended and thick. Remove from heat and gradually stir in milk, ¼ teaspoon salt, and pepper; stir until smooth. Return to heat, stirring constantly, until mixture is thick and bubbling. Pour evenly over the prepared cauliflower. Sprinkle bread crumbs and Parmesan cheese over top. Place in a 375° F. oven and bake for 15 to 20 minutes, or until lightly browned.

Makes 6 servings.

Peas in Cheese Sauce

SENSITIVITY CHECKLIST:

This recipe is   ____-free

_____✓_-free

____-free

____✓_-free

____✓_-free

Green beans or cut-up asparagus is delicious in this cheese sauce too. Add herbs such as parsley, chives, or dill for a variety of tastes.

2 packages (10 ounces each) frozen peas
1 tablespoon butter
1 tablespoon flour
¼ teaspoon salt
Dash of dry mustard
½ cup milk
½ cup grated Swiss cheese
½ cup diced white Cheddar cheese

Cook peas as directed on package. Drain. Melt butter in a large saucepan. Blend in flour, salt, and mustard. Stir in milk and cook over medium heat, stirring until thickened. Add Swiss and Cheddar cheese; heat until melted. Gently stir in peas and heat through.

Makes 8 servings.

Spinach in Citrus Sauce

SENSITIVITY CHECKLIST:

This recipe is
- dairy ——-free
- egg ——-free
- wheat ✔ -free
- corn ✔ -free
- sugar ✔ -free

If child has been placed on a natural salicylate-free diet omit orange juice in this recipe and double amount of lemon juice.

2 packages (10 ounces each) frozen chopped spinach
1 egg yolk
1½ teaspoons lemon juice
¼ cup butter, melted and hot
2 tablespoons orange juice

Cook spinach as directed on the package. Meanwhile, place egg yolk and lemon juice in a blender container; cover and run on low speed. While blender is running, remove cover and add a thin stream of the hot melted butter. When all the butter has been blended, turn off blender. Stir in orange juice. Drain cooked spinach and fold sauce through it.

Makes 6 servings.

Stewed Tomatoes

SENSITIVITY CHECKLIST:

This recipe is   ✓-free   *dairy*

✓-free   *egg*

✓-free   *wheat*

✓-free   *corn*

____-free   *sugar*

If the child has been placed on a natural salicylate-free diet, eliminate this recipe until permission has been granted to resume the use of tomatoes.

6 tomatoes, washed and quartered
1 onion, thinly sliced
½ teaspoon salt
¼ teaspoon pepper
1 teaspoon sugar
1 teaspoon lemon juice
½ cup water

Place tomatoes in a small heavy saucepan. Add sliced onion, salt, pepper, sugar, and lemon juice. Add water and cover tightly. Simmer for 20 minutes, stirring occasionally and adding more water if necessary to keep from sticking.

Makes 4 servings.

Broiled Tomatoes

This recipe is ____-free *dairy*

✓-free *egg*

✓-free *wheat*

✓-free *corn*

✓-free *sugar*

The trick with broiling tomatoes is to avoid overcooking, so tuck them into the broiler just before serving time for best results. Omit this recipe if child is on a natural salicylate-free diet.

6 tomatoes
¼ teaspoon salt
¼ teaspoon oregano
2 tablespoons grated Parmesan cheese
1 tablespoon butter

Wash tomatoes and cut in half. Arrange tomatoes cut sides up in a shallow baking dish. Sprinkle tops with salt, oregano, and cheese. Dot with butter. Broil for about 8 minutes or until topping is browned but tomatoes still hold shape.

Makes 6 servings.

Mashed Yellow Turnips

SENSITIVITY CHECKLIST:

This recipe is   _____-free
dairy

✓-free
egg

✓-free
wheat

✓-free
corn

✓-free
sugar

Here's a vegetable that is frequently overlooked despite the fact that it has a very appealing taste. It is especially good in this recipe.

1½ pounds yellow turnips, peeled and cut up
4 tablespoons butter
½ teaspoon grated lemon rind
½ teaspoon salt
¼ teaspoon mace
⅛ teaspoon pepper

Cook turnips in a small amount of water for about 20 minutes or until soft. Drain and mash. Add butter, lemon rind, salt, mace, and pepper, whipping well together.

Makes 4 to 6 servings.

Zucchini

SENSITIVITY CHECKLIST:

This recipe is   **dairy**   _____-free

egg   ✓-free

wheat   ✓-free

corn   ✓ free

sugar   ✓-free

Zucchini should be cooked fast to retain their crispness. For best taste, don't let them get overcooked and soggy.

2 pounds zucchini
1 teaspoon salt
¼ teaspoon thyme
2 tablespoons butter, melted
2 tablespoons lemon juice

Wash zucchini and trim off ends. Slice zucchini into ¼-inch circles. Place in a large skillet and cover with water. Add salt and thyme. Bring to a boil, cover and reduce heat to simmering. Cook about 5 minutes or until just tender. Drain. Combine melted butter and lemon juice; pour over zucchini and serve.

Makes 6 servings.

Mushroom Risotto.

SENSITIVITY CHECKLIST:

This recipe is ____-free *dairy*

✓-free *egg*

✓-free *wheat*

✓-free *corn*

✓-free *sugar*

Here's a perfect dish to serve with chicken or fish. Add a bit of saffron if natural yellow color is desired.

3 tablespoons butter
1 cup uncooked regular rice
½ cup chopped onion
½ cup diced green pepper
1 cup sliced fresh mushrooms
2 cups chicken broth (see Index)
1 teaspoon salt
½ cup grated Parmesan cheese

Melt butter in a large skillet; sauté rice until it glistens and becomes golden. Add onion, green pepper, and mushrooms. Continue cooking 5 minutes, stirring constantly to prevent overbrowning. Add chicken broth and salt. Bring to a boil and stir once. Cover, reduce heat, and simmer 15 minutes or until rice is tender and liquid is absorbed. Remove from heat. Toss lightly with cheese.

Makes 4 to 6 servings.

Potato Pancakes

SENSITIVITY CHECKLIST:

This recipe is  ___✓__-free

_____-free

_____-free

__✓__-free

__✓__-free

Grate potatoes just before frying or they will turn black. You can peel them several hours earlier though, if you soak them in cold salted water until ready to use. Child who has been placed on a natural salicylate-free diet should not be served applesauce with these pancakes, until permission has been granted to resume the use of apples.

2 pounds potatoes, pared
1 onion
1 egg, slightly beaten
2 tablespoons flour
½ teaspoon salt
¼ teaspoon pepper
1 cup peanut oil

Grate potatoes into a deep bowl. Grate onion and add to potatoes. Add beaten egg, flour, salt, and pepper. Heat oil in a large skillet. Drop large spoonfuls of mixture into the hot oil and fry as pancakes. Serve with applesauce or dairy sour cream.

Makes 6 servings.

Creamy Potato Salad

SENSITIVITY CHECKLIST:

This recipe is ____-free (dairy)

____-free (egg)

✓-free (wheat)

✓-free (corn)

✓-free (sugar)

Deliberately cook extra potatoes at dinnertime to have them on hand for this recipe the next day. Boil with skins on and peel later, for easiest and fastest way to remove peels.

2 pounds potatoes, cooked, pared, and cooled
2 scallions, thinly sliced
2 hard-cooked eggs, thinly sliced
2 stalks celery, thinly sliced
1 cup mayonnaise (see Index)
½ cup dairy sour cream
1 teaspoon salt
⅛ teaspoon pepper
2 tablespoons lemon juice

Cut potatoes into chunks and place in a large bowl. Add scallions, eggs, and celery; toss together. Combine mayonnaise, sour cream, salt, pepper, and lemon juice; mix thoroughly. Pour dressing over potatoes and toss lightly. Chill.

Makes 4 to 6 servings.

———

NOTE: If child is sensitive to corn oil, use other salad oil in preparing mayonnaise.

Coleslaw

SENSITIVITY CHECKLIST:

This recipe is   **✓**-free

    _____-free

    ✓-free

    ✓-free

    _____-free

This recipe can be adjusted to your personal taste. Add a little more sugar, a lot more onion, or mix the dressing with half mayonnaise and half dairy sour cream. Make it several hours ahead of time for best results.

1 medium head cabbage, shredded
2 carrots, grated
¼ green pepper, minced
1 cup mayonnaise (see Index)
1 tablespoon white vinegar
1 teaspoon salt
½ teaspoon sugar
⅛ teaspoon pepper
1 teaspoon grated onion

Combine cabbage, carrots, and green pepper in a bowl. Combine mayonnaise, vinegar, salt, sugar, pepper, and onion; mix thoroughly. Toss the mayonnaise mixture through the cabbage until well mixed. Cover and refrigerate until ready to serve.

Makes 8 servings.

NOTE: If child is sensitive to corn oil, use other salad oil in preparing mayonnaise.

Pickled Cucumbers and Onions

SENSITIVITY CHECKLIST:

This recipe is   ____✓____-free
                  dairy

                  ____✓____-free
                  egg

                  ____✓____-free
                  wheat

                  ____✓____-free
                  corn

                  _____-free
                  sugar

If child has been placed on a natural salicylate-free diet, omit this recipe until cucumbers are returned to list of allowable foods. Sugar may be omitted for those on sugar-free regime.

1 large or 2 small cucumbers
1 medium onion
½ cup white vinegar
¼ cup salad oil
1 teaspoon sugar
½ teaspoon salt
⅛ teaspoon pepper
¼ cup water

Pare cucumber and cut into paper-thin slices. Slice onion paper-thin and separate into rings. Place cucumber and onion in a small deep bowl or jar. Combine vinegar, oil, sugar, salt, and pepper; stir vigorously. Stir in water and immediately pour over cucumbers. Cover and refrigerate several hours or overnight.

Makes 4 to 6 servings.

Peanut Butter Vegetable Sauce

SENSITIVITY CHECKLIST:

This recipe is  ＿＿-free

dairy

✓-free

egg

＿＿-free

wheat

✓-free

corn

＿＿-free

sugar

Most commercial peanut butters are made with some sugar. Recipe can be made sugar-free by purchasing pure peanut butter in a health food store or making your own from roasted peanuts. Peanuts are a good source of protein. Check with your doctor for guidelines.

1 tablespoon butter
¼ cup creamy or chunk-style peanut butter
1 tablespoon flour
½ teaspoon salt
Dash pepper
1¼ cups milk

Melt butter in a small saucepan over medium heat. Mix in peanut butter until smooth, then add flour, salt, and pepper. Gradually stir in milk. Cook, stirring constantly, until mixture comes to boil. Reduce heat and simmer 1 minute. Serve over cauliflower, green beans, onions, or lima beans.

Makes 1 cup sauce.

Blender Mayonnaise

SENSITIVITY CHECKLIST:

This recipe is   **dairy**   ✓-free

           egg   _____-free

           wheat   ✓-free

           corn   ✓-free

           sugar   ✓-free

It's so easy to make your own mayonnaise that it's a wonder why more people don't do it. The trick is to drizzle the oil in a stream that forms an emulsified mixture. Then use this as a base for other salad dressings. Corn oil may be used if there is no sensitivity to it.

1 egg
½ teaspoon salt
2 tablespoons vinegar
1 cup salad oil

Break egg into electric blender container. Add salt and vinegar; blend. Add ⅓ cup salad oil; blend. Uncover, and blend while pouring the remaining salad oil in a steady stream. Turn off when all oil is absorbed. Makes 1¼ cups mayonnaise. Store in refrigerator in a tightly covered container.

Blender Hollandaise

SENSITIVITY CHECKLIST:

This recipe is

dairy _____-free

egg _____-free

wheat _✓_-free

corn _✓_-free

sugar _✓_-free

Since you can't use hollandaise sauce mixes that are obtainable in foil packets, you can make a superb sauce in your blender. Add a little more lemon juice if you prefer it that way.

¼ pound butter
2 egg yolks
2 teaspoons lemon juice
¼ teaspoon salt

Melt butter in a small saucepan. Place egg yolks in an electric blender; add lemon juice and salt. Blend on high and then turn to low and add melted butter a little at a time. Turn blender off at the last drop, as mixture gets creamy and thick. Refrigerate in a tightly covered jar for several days to use as needed. To reheat, stand jar in simmering water after bringing to room temperature.

Makes 1 cup sauce.

11

Pasta

Consider yourself lucky if your child is not sensitive to eggs or wheat, as pasta can provide a great deal of versatility to your menu planning. Most popular brands are a pure dried product with no artificial coloring or flavoring added. But it's important to read the labels to be sure. You'll find recipes in this chapter for making your own homemade noodles, and for making dough to put through a pasta machine in your own kitchen. It's the kind of project that the whole family can participate in—everyone enjoys the easy way the dough is placed into the machine and rolls out thin strands of delectable pasta.

Whichever way you decide to do it, there's a few tricks you might want to know about the best way of cooking pasta. A good rule of thumb is to boil at least four quarts of water for every pound of pasta that you plan to cook. Add a tablespoon of cooking oil to the salted water and you will eliminate the problem of stickiness when you drain the pasta after cooking. Cook until a strand tests "al dente"—just right to the bite, and then drain the pasta at once. If you have to hold the pasta for a while, mix sauce, butter, or broth through it to keep it from sticking. A good trick to use when making lasagne is to immerse the drained broad noodles into cold water after cooking. Slip each strand into a colander to dry for a moment before you add it to the layers of cheese and sauce.

Take a good look at the pasta section of your market to see what shapes, other than the popular spaghetti, macaroni, and noodles, are available to you. There are bows, shells, spirals, and large tubes for stuffing. All of these products may be kept safely on your kitchen shelf for an emergency family dinner.

If tomatoes have been deleted from your child's diet as part of a natural salicylate-free eating plan, don't despair. There are many other ways to serve pasta with equal gustatory pleasure, and you'll find a good number of them in this chapter to show you how it's done.

Naturally, you are restricted from using most prepared spaghetti sauces in cans, unless the labels convince you otherwise. Stay away from packaged dried spaghetti sauces and white sauces. And be sure that the cheese you use is white with no artificial additives added. The packaged dinners that contain pasta are also off limits, unless you find one that has natural ingredients only.

Despite these restrictions, you will find many ways to prepare pasta as a side dish for dinner or, if you add some form of protein to it, as a main dish for any meal. Your meals can be as interesting as your imagination can make them, and a choice of pasta is a good way to start.

Pasta

This recipe is **dairy** ___✓___-free

egg _____-free

wheat _____-free

corn ___✓___-free

sugar ___✓___-free

This dough may be used to make fettucini, spaghetti, or wide lasagne noodles. Be sure to let the dough rest for the prescribed time as it is easier to roll out. It is as fresh as pasta can get.

1¼ cups flour
2 eggs
¼ teaspoon salt
1 tablespoon water

Place flour in a mound on a pastry board. Make a hole in the center; break eggs into the hole. Add salt and water. Mix with fingers until well-blended into a dough, then knead until dough comes together easily, and leaves your hands clean of bits. Let dough rest, covered, for 1 hour. Divide dough into 8 pieces. Roll paper thin with pasta machine or by hand roller. Cut by machine into desired width of noodle or roll up and slice with a sharp knife. Spread out and dry for at least 20 minutes. Cook in boiling salted water for 10 minutes, or as directed in recipe.

Makes 4 servings.

Homemade Noodles

This recipe is

dairy   ✓-free

egg   ____-free

wheat   ____-free

corn   ✓-free

sugar   ✓-free

Noodles are so easy to make, you'll wonder why you haven't tried it before. It's even easier if you have a small pasta-making machine.

1 egg
2 tablespoons water
½ teaspoon salt
½ cup flour

Beat egg, water, and salt together. Slowly add flour until a soft dough is formed. Roll dough out thin and let dry for about 20 minutes. Then roll dough up jelly-roll fashion, and slice thin. Spread noodles out to dry. To cook, drop in boiling water for 10 minutes.

Fettucini Alfredo

SENSITIVITY CHECKLIST:

This recipe is   _____-free

                   _____-free

                   _____-free

                   ✓-free

                   ✓-free

This is the way this famous dish is prepared at the original Alfredo's Restaurant in Rome. It's supposed to be bland and rich with dairy products. A perfect answer for the child who enjoys pasta but cannot have a tomato sauce due to a natural salicylate-free diet.

1 package (8 ounces) medium noodles (no additives) or 1 recipe pasta (see Index)
¼ cup cream
½ cup butter
¼ cup grated Parmesan cheese

Cook pasta in boiling salted water 10 minutes. Drain. Toss with cream, bits of butter, and grated cheese. Serve at once.

Makes 4 servings.

Spaghetti Milanese

SENSITIVITY CHECKLIST:

This recipe is ☐ **dairy** __✓__-free

○ **egg** _____-free

wheat _____-free

corn __✓__-free

sugar __✓__-free

If child has been placed on a natural salicylate-free diet, omit this recipe until permission has been granted to resume the use of tomatoes. This is a meal-in-one if extra chicken livers are added.

¼ cup olive oil
1 large onion, diced
1 cup sliced mushrooms
2 cloves garlic, minced
8 chicken livers
1 teaspoon oregano
½ teaspoon salt
¼ teaspoon pepper
2 cans (1 pound each) Italian tomatoes
1 pound spaghetti

Heat oil in a skillet. Add diced onion, sliced mushrooms, and minced garlic; sauté until onions are golden. Cut chicken livers into small chunks; add to skillet and brown on all sides. Add oregano, salt, and pepper. Add tomatoes, breaking with the side of a spoon. Simmer for 15 minutes. Meanwhile, cook spaghetti as directed on package. Drain. Pour onto a warm platter. Pour sauce over and toss lightly to coat the pasta. Serve at once.

Makes 6 servings.

Spaghetti with White Clam Sauce

SENSITIVITY CHECKLIST:

This recipe is   _✓_-free
dairy

       _____-free
egg

       _____-free
wheat

       _✓_-free
corn

       _✓_-free
sugar

Check labels on pasta package and on canned clams. This is a very tasty tomato-free way of serving the spaghetti that children love to eat.

2 cans minced clams
½ cup olive oil
3 cloves garlic, minced
2 tablespoons chopped parsley
½ teaspoon salt
¼ teaspoon pepper
1 pound spaghetti

Drain clams. Heat olive oil in a skillet. Add garlic and brown lightly. Add parsley, clams, salt, and pepper. Stir and simmer several minutes; remove from heat. Meanwhile, cook spaghetti according to package directions. Drain. Pour onto a warm platter and pour clam sauce over. Toss lightly and serve at once.

Makes 6 servings.

Spaghetti with Tomato-Meat Sauce

SENSITIVITY CHECKLIST:

This recipe is   ___✓___-free   *dairy*

_____-free   *egg*

_____-free   *wheat*

___✓___-free   *corn*

___✓___-free   *sugar*

If child has been placed on a natural salicylate-free diet, omit this recipe until permission has been granted to resume the use of tomatoes. Check labels on pasta package and canned tomatoes to be sure that no artificial additives are listed in the ingredients.

3 tablespoons olive oil
1 large onion, diced
1 green pepper, diced
½ pound ground beef
2 cans (1 pound each) Italian tomatoes
1 can (6 ounces) tomato paste
1 teaspoon salt
¼ teaspoon pepper
½ teaspoon oregano
1 pound spaghetti

Heat oil in a large skillet. Sauté onion and green pepper. Add ground beef and break into tiny bits with a fork; brown well. Stir in tomatoes and tomato paste. Add salt, pepper, and oregano. Simmer, covered, for 1 hour. Fifteen minutes before you are ready to serve, cook spaghetti according to directions on package. Drain. Place on a warm platter and pour tomato-meat sauce over pasta. Serve at once.

Makes 6 servings.

Green Noodles with Spinach Sauce

SENSITIVITY CHECKLIST:

This recipe is   ✓-free *dairy*

                  _____-free *egg*

                  _____-free *wheat*

                  ✓-free *corn*

                  ✓-free *sugar*

Be sure to read the label on the green noodle package to be sure that only spinach has been used to color the noodles, and that it contains no artificial additives. This is another interesting way to serve noodles when tomatoes have been removed from the diet.

1 package (1 pound) green noodles
12 spinach leaves
4 sprigs parsley
½ cup grated Parmesan cheese
2 cloves garlic, peeled
½ teaspoon salt
½ cup broken walnuts
¼ cup olive oil
¼ cup hot water

Cook green noodles as directed on package; drain. Place all other ingredients into an electric blender and process into a fine sauce. Pour over cooked noodles and serve at once.

Makes 6 servings.

Noodle Pudding

SENSITIVITY CHECKLIST:

This recipe is ____-free (dairy)

____-free (egg)

____-free (wheat)

✓-free (corn)

✓-free (sugar)

If the child has been placed on a natural salicylate-free diet do not add raisins to this recipe. Instead add drained pineapple tidbits or any other permissible fruit.

1 package (8 ounces) broad noodles
3 eggs
½ pound creamed cottage cheese
1 cup dairy sour cream
¼ teaspoon salt
½ cup white seedless raisins
⅓ cup butter
¼ cup bread crumbs (see Index)

Preheat oven to 350° F. Cook noodles according to package directions, or boil in salted water for about 8 minutes until tender. Drain. Beat eggs. Add cottage cheese, sour cream, salt, and raisins. Fold noodles into this mixture. Put half of the butter in a 7½-by-12-inch baking dish. Heat in the oven until butter is melted, then pour in noodle mixture. Dot top with remaining butter and bread crumbs. Bake for 1 hour. This pudding may be baked in greased muffin tins for approximately 30 minutes, and served in individual portions. The leftover noodle muffins may be frozen in a plastic bag and reheated in the muffin tin at a later date.

Makes 6 servings.

Lasagne

SENSITIVITY CHECKLIST:

This recipe is ____-free

dairy

____-free

egg

____-free

wheat

✓-free

corn

✓-free

sugar

If child has been placed on a natural salicylate-free diet, omit this recipe until permission has been granted to resume the use of tomatoes. Remember that pasta is usually made with eggs, in case an egg-free diet has been prescribed.

1 pound ground beef
2 tablespoons olive oil
1 large onion, chopped
2 cloves garlic, finely chopped
1 teaspoon basil
1 teaspoon oregano
½ teaspoon salt
1 can (30 ounces) tomatoes
1 can (6 ounces) tomato paste
½ pound lasagne noodles
2 cups ricotta cheese
½ pound mozzarella cheese, thinly sliced
½ cup grated Parmesan cheese

Brown beef slowly in oil. Add onion and continue cooking until onion is transparent, stirring frequently. Add garlic, basil, and oregano, and cook a few minutes longer, stirring constantly. Add salt, tomatoes, and tomato paste. Simmer for 1 hour. When almost done, cook lasagne noodles in boiling salted water for 20 minutes; drain and rinse. Spoon a layer of sauce into a flat 8-by-12-inch baking dish. Arrange a layer of noodles side-by-side over sauce. Spread with a layer of half the ricotta cheese. Top with thin slices of mozzarella cheese and sprinkle with Parmesan cheese. Repeat layers. Top with noodles. Spread remaining sauce over noodles. Dot with remaining mozzarella cheese. Sprinkle with Parmesan cheese. Bake in a 350° F. oven for 45 minutes.

Makes 6 to 8 servings.

Noodle Bows and Cheese

SENSITIVITY CHECKLIST:

This recipe is   ____-free
dairy

____-free
egg

____-free
wheat

✓-free
corn

✓-free
sugar

This recipe is one that most children love and is chockful of high dairy protein. Not for any child who is sensitive to dairy products. Most pasta is made with eggs. If the child is sensitive to eggs, perhaps you can find a brand that is egg-free.

1 package (1 pound) noodle bows (no artificial additives)
2 tablespoons butter
1 cup freshly grated Parmesan cheese
1 cup diced Swiss cheese
1 cup diced mozzarella cheese
3 tablespoons butter
3 tablespoons flour
3 cups milk
1 teaspoon salt
¼ teaspoon pepper
⅛ teaspoon nutmeg

Cook noodle bows in boiling water according to package directions. Drain in colander. Toss with 2 tablespoons butter. Add cheeses and toss again to mix well. In a saucepan, melt butter and blend in flour until smooth and thick. Gradually add milk; cook, stirring constantly, until sauce boils 1 minute. Add salt, pepper, and nutmeg. Turn half the noodle-cheese mixture into a buttered baking dish; top with half of the sauce. Repeat layers. Sprinkle extra grated Parmesan on top. Bake in a 350° F. oven for 25 minutes. Serve at once. Makes 6 servings.

Baked Macaroni and Cheese

SENSITIVITY CHECKLIST:

This recipe is ____-free (dairy)

____-free (egg)

____-free (wheat)

✓-free (corn)

✓-free (sugar)

This dish can easily be turned into a main course with the addition of flaked fish and cooked vegetables. Either way, it is a family favorite.

2 tablespoons butter
2 tablespoons flour
½ teaspoon salt
¼ teaspoon pepper
2 cups milk
2 cups diced white Cheddar or Swiss cheese
1 pound macaroni

In a saucepan, melt butter and stir in flour, salt, and pepper until smooth and thick. Remove from heat; stir in milk until smooth. Return to heat and cook, stirring constantly, until sauce is bubbling and thickened. Add cheese and stir until melted. Meanwhile, cook macaroni as directed on package. Drain. Lightly grease a casserole and pour hot sauce into it. Stir in cooked macaroni. Bake for 20 minutes in a 350° F. oven. Serve hot.

Makes 6 servings.

Macaroni and Egg Salad

SENSITIVITY CHECKLIST:

This recipe is

dairy ✓-free

egg _____-free

wheat ✓-free

corn ✓-free

sugar ✓-free

This is a good lunchbox item to be carried to school in a wide thermos jar. Tuck in several thin slices of roast beef for extra protein; roll each around a carrot stick and wrap in aluminum foil.

4 teaspoons salt
3 quarts boiling water
2 cups elbow macaroni (8 ounces)
½ cup chopped celery
¼ cup chopped Bermuda onion
¼ teaspoon dill
⅛ teaspoon pepper
3 tablespoons vinegar
2 tablespoons salad oil
4 hard-cooked eggs
⅔ cup mayonnaise (see Index)
Lettuce leaves

Add 3 teaspoons salt to rapidly boiling water. Add macaroni gradually so that the water continues to boil. Cook, uncovered, stirring occasionally, until tender. Drain. Rinse with cold water; drain again. Mix macaroni, celery, onion, 1 teaspoon salt, dill, pepper, vinegar, and oil in a large bowl. Chill. Coarsely chop eggs and add with mayonnaise to the chilled macaroni mixture; mix lightly. Serve on lettuce.

Makes 4 servings.

———

NOTE: If child is sensitive to corn oil, use other salad oil in preparing mayonnaise.

12

Eggs

If your child is not sensitive to eggs, you can depend on them to ease your budget when planning high-protein meals. Remember to keep rotating the menu every four days, using eggs for only one of those twelve meals. Bits of leftover vegetables and cheese may be combined into a delicious omelet in just a matter of minutes for other members of the family at any time, so you may want to have a few pointers to help you to cook eggs better from now on.

1. Always cook eggs over low heat so they don't get tough.
2. Eggs separate better when they are cold, but the whites beat higher when they are at room temperature. A few grains of salt will expand the volume of beaten egg whites.
3. To boil eggs, choose a saucepan that won't darken (aluminum always does) and one that is deep enough so that water will cover the eggs completely but still not splash over during cooking.
4. To boil eggs, bring the water to a boil first, and then reduce the heat to a low simmer. Place eggs in the water with a slotted spoon. Cook soft-cooked eggs for 2 to 4 minutes, depending on how solid you prefer them. Cook hard-cooked eggs for 12 to 15 minutes. Rinse immediately under cold water and the shells will slip off with no trouble at all.

5.   To poach eggs, use a skillet full of boiling water. Add a teaspoon of vinegar to the water and reduce the heat. Stir a circle in the water and break an egg into the circle; push the spreading white back over the yolk with a spoon until it solidifies. Cook for about 4 minutes. Remove egg with a slotted spoon and serve on toast or an English muffin half.

6.   To fry eggs, heat butter in a skillet until melted. Break each egg carefully into the skillet and cook until done the way you like it. Turn over with a spatula if you prefer your egg done on both sides, or just spoon a bit of white over the yolk and place a cover over the pan for a moment until a thin film forms. Remove egg with a spatula.

7.   To scramble eggs, heat butter in a skillet and pour in beaten eggs. Let egg mixture solidify around the edges and then gently push the cooked egg toward the center to permit the uncooked portion to flow around the edges and set. Avoid any vigorous stirring as the mixture will crumble into tiny particles. Remove from heat when the mixture is still moist, or it will be overcooked by the time you serve it.

8.   Cover leftover raw egg whites and refrigerate for several days. Place leftover raw egg yolks in a small container, cover with water and refrigerate covered for several days, or poach yolks in boiling water and sieve them as a flavorful garnish over cooked vegetables.

Here are some easy egg recipes with some exciting new twists. They are designed to help you create combinations of your own.

Creamy Scrambled Eggs

SENSITIVITY CHECKLIST:

This recipe is _____-free (dairy)

_____-free (egg)

__✓__-free (wheat)

__✓__-free (corn)

__✓__-free (sugar)

The secret of scrambling eggs well is to remove from heat as soon as all of the mixture solidifies, even though it still has a wet look. Vary the herb used, to get a different flavor every time.

1 tablespoon butter
4 eggs
¼ teaspoon salt
⅛ teaspoon pepper
⅛ teaspoon thyme
½ cup dairy sour cream

Melt butter in a large skillet. Beat eggs, salt, pepper, and thyme together until well blended. Pour into skillet. Stir in sour cream. Cook over very low heat, stirring occasionally, until eggs reach desired firmness. Serve at once.

Makes 2 to 3 servings.

Cheese Scrambled Eggs

SENSITIVITY CHECKLIST:

This recipe is

_____-free

dairy

_____-free

egg

✓-free

wheat

✓-free

corn

✓-free

sugar

Be sure to use the uncolored cheese. Add a sprinkling of herbs–chives, fresh parsley, or tarragon–for variety and good taste.

4 eggs
2 tablespoons milk
¼ teaspoon salt
1 tablespoon butter
2 slices white Cheddar cheese

Beat together eggs, milk, and salt. Melt butter in a skillet; pour in the egg mixture. Reduce heat just enough to cook eggs quickly, pushing the cooked portions of the egg toward the center so the liquid portion will run off to the sides. When eggs are done as desired, top with cheese and cover skillet for a moment until cheese melts. Serve at once.

Makes 2 or 3 servings.

Cottage Scrambled Eggs

SENSITIVITY CHECKLIST:

This recipe is   ____-free   *dairy*

____-free   *egg*

✓-free   *wheat*

✓-free   *corn*

✓-free   *sugar*

Here's a quick breakfast to stir up that will give high protein energy all the way until lunch. Serves four with only one skillet to wash.

½ cup creamed cottage cheese
1 tablespoon chopped chives
8 eggs
¼ cup milk
½ teaspoon salt
2 tablespoons butter

Mix together cottage cheese and chives; set aside. Beat together eggs, milk, and salt lightly with a fork. Melt butter in a skillet; pour in the egg mixture. Reduce heat just enough to cook eggs quickly, pushing the cooked portions of egg toward the center so the liquid portion will run off to the sides. When eggs are almost done, quickly stir in the cottage cheese mixture. Heat for a moment and then serve at once.

Makes 4 servings.

Jam Scramble

SENSITIVITY CHECKLIST:

This recipe is

dairy   _____-free

egg   _____-free

wheat   _✓_-free

corn   _✓_-free

sugar   _____-free

Look for pure jellies and jams at your local health food store. Check the labels to be sure there are no artificial colors or flavorings. Omit recipe for those children on a sugar-free regime. Children who have been placed on a natural salicylate-free diet should not be served preserves made from fruits on that list (see chapter 3).

4 eggs
¼ cup milk
½ teaspoon salt
1 teaspoon butter
2 tablespoons pure strawberry jam (or your favorite flavor)

Beat together eggs, milk, and salt lightly with a fork. Melt butter in a skillet; pour in the egg mixture. Reduce heat just enough to cook eggs quickly, pushing the cooked portions of egg toward the center so the liquid portion will run off to the sides. Drop teaspoonfuls of strawberry jam here and there over top of eggs; stir in slightly with the tip of a fork. Serve at once.

Makes 2 servings.

Onion-Pepper Omelet

SENSITIVITY CHECKLIST:

This recipe is ____-free

dairy

____-free

egg

✔-free

wheat

✔-free

corn

✔-free

sugar

If child is not on a natural salicylate-free diet, you may add a chopped fresh tomato to the skillet and cook for several minutes before pouring egg mixture over all. With this kind of omelet, the filling is cooked right into the egg.

3 tablespoons butter
1 onion, thinly sliced
1 green pepper, seeded and diced
4 eggs
1 tablespoon cold water
¼ teaspoon salt

Melt butter in a skillet. Add onions and green pepper; sauté until limp. Beat eggs well; add water and salt. Pour eggs over onions and pepper and cook until solidified. With a spatula, roll omelet out of the pan onto a warm platter.

Makes 2 servings.

Poached Eggs on English Muffin

SENSITIVITY CHECKLIST:

This recipe is

_____-free

_____-free

_____-free

✓-free

✓-free

Metal rings are available in housewares departments to keep the poaching eggs in place. Just slip each egg into the center of a ring, after the water has come to a boil.

1 teaspoon vinegar
4 eggs
2 English muffins, cut in half
Salt

Fill a skillet with water. Add vinegar and heat to a rolling boil. Reduce heat to keep water simmering. Break 1 egg into a saucer; then make a circle in the simmering water with a spoon and quickly slip the egg into the center of the circle. Repeat with the remaining eggs, one at a time. Use the spoon to deftly fold all wisps of egg white onto the egg, trying to keep each egg in a perfect circle as it cooks. Cook 3 to 4 minutes, depending on desired doneness. Remove each egg with a slotted spoon and place on a half of toasted muffin. Salt as desired. Serve at once.

Makes 4 servings.

Eggs Florentine

SENSITIVITY CHECKLIST:

This recipe is   _____-free   dairy

_____-free   egg

✓-free   wheat

_____-free   corn

✓-free   sugar

This is a good lunch or supper dish. If child has a sensitivity to corn, wheat flour may be substituted for cornstarch. This recipe works well with asparagus spears too.

4 tablespoons butter
¼ cup chopped onion
1 package (10 ounces) frozen chopped spinach, cooked and drained
1 tablespoon cornstarch
½ cup milk
4 hard-cooked eggs, cut in half
2 cups White Sauce (recipe follows)
½ cup fine dry bread crumbs (see Index)
2 tablespoons grated Parmesan cheese

Melt 2 tablespoons butter in 1½-quart saucepan over medium heat. Sauté onion, stirring frequently, until tender. Add spinach. Mix cornstarch and milk. Stir into spinach. Bring to a boil, stirring constantly, and boil 1 minute. Turn into a 10-by-6-by-1¾-inch baking dish. Place egg halves on top. Cover with White Sauce. Toss bread crumbs and cheese with 2 tablespoons melted butter. Sprinkle over egg mixture. Bake in 350° F. oven about 20 minutes or until casserole is heated through and bread crumbs are browned.

Makes 4 servings.

White Sauce

This recipe is

dairy ____-free

egg ✔-free

wheat ✔-free

corn ____-free

sugar ✔-free

4 tablespoons butter
2 tablespoons cornstarch
1 teaspoon salt
¼ teaspoon pepper
2 cups milk

Melt butter in a small saucepan. Mix in cornstarch, salt, and pepper. Remove from heat. Gradually add milk, stirring until smooth. Cook over medium heat, stirring constantly, until mixture comes to a boil and boils 1 minute.

Makes 2 cups.

Baked Egg in a Muffin

SENSITIVITY CHECKLIST:

This recipe is   **✔**-free
     dairy

       ____-free
     egg

       ____-free
     wheat

       ✔-free
     corn

       ✔-free
     sugar

This is a good egg trick when you have a lot of people to feed and want to do some preparations in advance. Eggs can be in muffins and refrigerated until ready to use within a few hours. A great brunch idea.

½ English muffin
1 egg
Dash of salt
Dash of pepper

Scoop out soft center of the English muffin half. Place on a baking pan. Break egg carefully into the muffin cup. Sprinkle with salt and pepper. Bake in a 350° F. oven for about 15 minutes, or until egg reaches desired firmness. Serve at once.

Makes 1 serving.

Puffy Egg Squares

SENSITIVITY CHECKLIST:

This recipe is   **dairy** ____-free

egg ____-free

wheat ✓-free

corn ____-free

sugar ✓-free

This recipe is a weekend morning treat. For a change of pace, add several tablespoons of chopped chives to the mixture before baking.

2 tablespoons butter
3 tablespoons cornstarch
½ teaspoon salt
⅛ teaspoon pepper
1 cup milk
4 egg yolks, slightly beaten
4 egg whites, stiffly beaten

Melt butter in saucepan. Remove from heat; stir in cornstarch, salt, and pepper. Gradually stir in milk until smooth. Bring to a boil over medium heat, stirring constantly, and boil 1 minute. Remove from heat and pour gradually over egg yolks, mixing well. Fold egg yolk mixture into egg whites. Pour into an ungreased 8-inch-square pan. Place in pan of warm water and bake in a 350° F. oven 45 to 50 minutes or until knife inserted in center comes out clean. Cut into squares and serve immediately.

Makes 4 to 6 servings.

Toad-in-the-hole

SENSITIVITY CHECKLIST:

This recipe is   _____-free
     dairy

_____-free
egg

_____-free
wheat

✓-free
corn

✓-free
sugar

Children will probably giggle over the name of this recipe and love the taste of it too. If permitted, spread a little allowable jelly over top of bread before breaking egg into center.

1 slice bread
3 tablespoons butter
1 egg
⅛ teaspoon salt

Tear a circle out of the center of the bread slice and use for another purpose. Melt butter in a skillet and fry bread on one side until lightly browned. Turn bread over and break egg into the hole of the bread. Sprinkle with salt. Fry until egg is solidified and bottom of bread is lightly browned. Serve at once.

Makes 1 serving.

Deviled Eggs

This recipe is

           _____-free

           _____-free

           _✓_-free

           _✓_-free

           _✓_-free

If child is placed on a dairy-free diet, omit sour cream and substitute homemade mayonnaise (see Index).

6 peeled hard-boiled eggs
1 tablespoon dairy sour cream
¼ teaspoon salt
⅛ teaspoon dry mustard
⅛ teaspoon pepper
⅛ teaspoon paprika

Cut eggs in half lengthwise. Scoop out the yolks and place in a bowl, reserving the whites. Mash the yolks; add sour cream, salt, dry mustard, and pepper, mixing well. Spoon mixture back into the reserved whites, mounding the yolks carefully in their cavities. Sprinkle paprika over the yolks. Chill until ready to serve.

Makes 12 deviled eggs.

French Toast

SENSITIVITY CHECKLIST:

This recipe is _____-free
dairy

_____-free
egg

_____-free
wheat

✓-free
corn

✓-free
sugar

The rest of the family might want to sprinkle a little confectioners' sugar on this. Once in a while, the hyperactive child may do so too, providing a sugar-free regime has not been prescribed. If serving maple syrup, be sure that it is the pure variety completely free of artificial color and flavorings.

2 eggs
1 cup milk
¼ teaspoon salt
¼ teaspoon baking powder
8 slices thick day-old bread (no artificial additives)
2 tablespoons butter

Beat together eggs and milk until frothy. Mix in salt and baking powder. Dip bread slices into this batter until well soaked. Melt butter in a large skillet or griddle. Place bread slices in melted butter and cook until brown on one side; turn and brown the other side. Serve at once.

Makes 4 servings.

———

NOTE: Mix the batter the night before; cover tightly and refrigerate for an early start.

Blender Banana Egg Nog

SENSITIVITY CHECKLIST:

This recipe is   ____-free

____-free

_✓_-free

_✓_-free

_✓_-free

This makes a nourishing breakfast drink for finicky eaters or an after-school treat that isn't sweet.

1 very ripe banana, cut into chunks
1 egg
1 cup cold milk
½ teaspoon pure vanilla extract

Place banana chunks in blender container and blend until mashed. Add egg; blend again. Add milk and vanilla and blend until frothy. Serve at once.

Makes 1 large serving.

_____

NOTE: If you don't have an electric blender, beat all ingredients with a rotary beater or electric mixer.

Cheese Blintzes

SENSITIVITY CHECKLIST:

This recipe is   _____-free
dairy

_____-free
egg

_____-free
wheat

✓-free
corn

✓-free
sugar

If child is not on a completely sugar-free regime, you may want to add a teaspoon of sugar to the filling mixture. Blintzes may be made earlier in the day and refrigerated until ready to brown and serve. They may also be frozen and kept for several weeks; thaw in refrigerator before browning.

BATTER
½ cup flour
½ teaspoon salt
2 eggs, well beaten
⅔ cup milk
1 tablespoon melted butter

Sift flour, add salt, and sift again. Combine eggs, milk, and melted butter. Add flour slowly to egg batter and beat until smooth.

FILLING
½ pound farmer cheese
½ pound cream cheese
1 egg, well beaten
2 tablespoons melted butter
1 teaspoon pure vanilla extract
¼ teaspoon cinnamon

Mash the farmer cheese and cream cheese together. Add beaten egg, melted butter, vanilla, and cinnamon. Blend well. To make blintzes, brush a 6-inch skillet lightly with melted butter, heat it, and pour in just enough batter to cover the bottom of the skillet. Cook until firm and turn out on a clean dish towel, browning only one side of the crepe. When all the batter is used up, fill each crepe with about 2 tablespoons of filling, placing the filling on the center of the browned side of the crepe and folding over the two opposite sides; then roll up the remaining sides to enclose the filling in the crepe. Brown in butter just before serving. Serve with sour cream, if desired.

Makes 1 dozen.

13

Breads, Biscuits, and Muffins

Here's an area of the hyperactive child's menu that can get out of hand very easily, especially if there is a sensitivity to wheat. It's certain that you have enough to do without having to bake your own bread too. If you can find bread that is all natural, that will solve the average child's problems. But if there is a special sensitivity you will have to go to a health food store to try to find an egg-free, dairy-free, or wheat-free bread, or decide to bake your own.

It's a good idea to double up when baking and freeze as much as you can for the days when you haven't time or are not in the mood to bake bread. Here is one item of food that is best kept for the special child, letting the rest of the family eat other bread, or else you may be baking several times a week.

You'll find many unique breads, biscuits, and muffins in this chapter to give you a variety of grains and tastes. Some are made with yeast dough, but most are a quick-stir kind that are easy to do.

You'll need some muffin pans and loaf pans to be able to freeze extra quantities. Be sure to purchase the heaviest metal that you can, for durability and a good bread product. Use a pastry brush to spread oil; it permits you to use only a small amount and will cover the surface more evenly.

It helps to have an electric mixer with a dough hook for those breads that need to be kneaded, or at least a hand mixer for the quick breads that don't. Wrap cooled bread in heavy-duty aluminum foil to freeze, and mark carefully with the date of baking so you can use up the oldest bread first. Home-baked breads will stay fresher longer if you pop them into plastic bags and store in the refrigerator after the first day.

Don't overlook the possibility of turning browning bananas into a healthful tea bread, or of adding raisins (not for the child on a natural salicylate-free diet) or nuts to many of the other tea breads and muffins you will find. Whatever your approach turns out to be, here's a chapter of recipes that will be dependable and delicious. You'll find several for each special sensitivity that you may be coping with too.

White Bread

This recipe is _____-free (dairy)

✓-free (egg)

_____-free (wheat)

✓-free (corn)

_____-free (sugar)

7¾ to 8¾ cups unsifted flour
3 tablespoons sugar
½ teaspoon salt
3 packages active dry yeast
⅓ cup butter
2⅔ cups very warm water
Peanut oil

In a large bowl thoroughly mix 3 cups flour, sugar, salt, and undis-solved yeast. Add butter. Gradually add warm water to dry ingredients and beat with an electric mixer 2 minutes at medium speed, scraping the bowl occasionally. Add ½ cup flour. Beat at high speed 2 minutes, scraping bowl occasionally. Stir in enough additional flour to make a stiff dough. Turn out onto a lightly floured breadboard; knead until smooth and elastic (about 10 to 12 minutes). Cover with plastic wrap, then a towel. Let rest 20 minutes. Divide dough in half. Roll each half into a 9-by-14-inch rectangle. Shape into loaves by rolling the upper short side towards you. Seal with thumbs. Seal ends; fold sealed ends under. Be careful not to tear the dough. Grease two 9-by-5-by-3-inch loaf pans with butter. Place the loaves in the pans seam side down. Brush with peanut oil. Cover loosely with plastic wrap. Refrigerate 2 to 24 hours. When ready to bake, remove from refrigerator and uncover dough carefully. Let stand at room temperature 10 minutes. Puncture any gas bubbles which may have formed with a greased toothpick or metal skewer. Bake in a 400° F. oven for 35 to 40 minutes or until done. Remove from baking pans and cool on wire racks. Loaves may be frozen for future use.

Makes 2 loaves.

Apricot Bran Bread

SENSITIVITY CHECKLIST:

This recipe is   ____-free   *dairy*

____-free   *egg*

____-free   *wheat*

__✓__-free   *corn*

____-free   *sugar*

If child has been placed on a natural salicylate-free diet, omit this recipe until permission has been granted to resume the use of apricots. If child has a strict sugar-free regime, omit this recipe.

1 cup finely cut dried apricots
1½ cups boiling water
¾ cup sugar
1½ cups whole-bran cereal
1 cup milk
2 eggs, slightly beaten
⅓ cup salad oil
1½ cups sifted flour
1 tablespoon baking powder
1 teaspoon salt
1 tablespoon sugar

Preheat oven to 350° F. Cover apricots with boiling water; let stand 10 minutes and drain well. Mix apricots and ¾ cup sugar; set aside. Combine bran cereal and milk in a large bowl; let stand a minute or two until most of the liquid is absorbed. Add eggs and oil and beat well. Sift together flour, baking powder, and salt; add to cereal mixture, stirring only until all ingredients are moistened. Fold in apricot mixture. Spread batter evenly in a well-greased 9-by-5-inch loaf pan lined with waxed paper. Sprinkle top with 1 tablespoon sugar. Bake for 1 hour, or until wooden pick inserted near center comes out clean. Let stand until thoroughly cooled before slicing.

Makes 1 loaf.

Peanut Butter Yeast Bread

SENSITIVITY CHECKLIST:

This recipe is   ____-free
dairy

✓-free
egg

____-free
wheat

✓-free
corn

____-free
sugar

This is a nicely flavored bread for everyone, but especially for those who are sensitive to eggs. Sugar may be omitted by those who are on a completely sugar-free regime, although if the bread is cut into 18 slices there is only ⅓ teaspoon of sugar in each slice. Check label on peanut butter to avoid high sugar content there. If necessary purchase in a health food store or make your own.

1 cup milk
2 tablespoons sugar
2 teaspoons salt
3 tablespoons salad oil
1 cup warm water
1 package active dry yeast, or 1 cake compressed yeast
6 cups sifted flour, approximately
½ cup creamy or chunk-style peanut butter
2 tablespoons melted butter

Scald milk, then stir in sugar, salt, and salad oil. Cool to lukewarm. Measure water into warm mixing bowl. Sprinkle or crumble in yeast and stir until dissolved. Blend in lukewarm milk mixture. Add 3 cups flour; beat until smooth. Add remaining flour or enough to make an easily handled dough. Turn out dough onto a lightly floured board or cloth. Let rest 15 minutes. Knead until smooth and elastic. Place in oiled bowl, smooth side down. Then turn ball of dough so smooth side is up. (This lightly greases the top.) Cover with clean towel. Let rise in warm place, free from draft, until doubled in bulk, about 1 hour and 20 minutes. Punch down. Roll out on lightly floured board to 12-inch square. Spread with peanut butter. Roll up. Pinch dough to seal edge. Bring ends together and overlap side by side about one inch, forming a ring. Tuck inside end into center; seal. Tuck outside end under ring from outside. Place on ungreased cookie sheet. Cover; let rise as directed above until doubled in bulk, about 45 minutes. Brush with melted butter. Score top with knife, making 1½-inch squares. Bake in a 400° F. oven until brown and crusty, about 40 minutes.

Makes 1 large loaf.

Rye Bread

SENSITIVITY CHECKLIST:

This recipe is

dairy _✓_-free

egg ____-free

wheat _✓_-free

corn _✓_-free

sugar ____-free

This is an easy version of a yeast-raised rye bread–here, just a good mixing is required before popping the bread into the oven. So good, maybe you should be baking two at a time and freezing one.

2 cups rye flour
2 tablespoons sugar
3 tablespoons baking powder
½ teaspoon salt
3 eggs, slightly beaten
½ cup water
2 teaspoons salad oil

Preheat oven to 350° F. Sift together rye flour, sugar, baking powder, and salt; add eggs, water, and oil and beat thoroughly. Pour into a greased loaf pan and bake 40 minutes, or until lightly browned.

Makes 1 loaf.

Walnut Cheddar Bread

This recipe is  _____-free

_____-free

_____-free

✓-free

_____-free

Be sure that the Cheddar cheese is the white color—you may have to shop for it in a cheese specialty store. It makes a nice nourishing loaf of bread.

2½ cups sifted all-purpose flour
2 tablespoons sugar
2 teaspoons baking powder
1¼ teaspoons salt
½ teaspoon dry mustard
½ teaspoon baking soda
Dash cayenne
¼ cup butter
1 cup grated white Cheddar cheese
1 egg
1 cup buttermilk
½ teaspoon pure Worcestershire sauce
1 cup chopped walnuts

Resift flour with sugar, baking powder, salt, mustard, baking soda, and cayenne. Cut in butter. Add cheese, and mix in with a fork. Beat egg lightly; add buttermilk and Worcestershire sauce. Stir into dry mixture just until moistened. Add walnuts and mix well. Turn the stiff dough into a greased 8½-by-4½-inch loaf pan and smooth top. Bake in a 350° F. oven for 55 minutes. Let stand 10 minutes, then turn out and cool on wire rack.

Makes 1 loaf.

Cinnamon-Raisin Bread

SENSITIVITY CHECKLIST:

This recipe is ____-free (dairy)

____-free (egg)

____-free (wheat)

__✓__-free (corn)

____-free (sugar)

If child has been placed on a natural salicylate-free diet, omit the raisins and do not use almonds for chopped nuts.

1 cup sifted all-purpose flour
2½ teaspoons baking powder
½ teaspoon salt
1 teaspoon cinnamon
1 cup whole-bran cereal
¾ cup milk
½ cup butter
½ cup sugar
2 eggs
1 cup seedless raisins
½ cup chopped nuts
2 tablespoons sugar
¼ teaspoon cinnamon

Sift together flour, baking powder, salt, and 1 teaspoon cinnamon; set aside. Combine cereal and milk; let stand until most of moisture is absorbed. Beat butter and ½ cup sugar until fluffy. Add eggs and beat well. Stir in cereal mixture, raisins, and nuts. Add sifted dry ingredients, stirring until combined. Spread in a greased 9-inch layer cake pan. Mix 2 tablespoons sugar and ¼ teaspoon cinnamon for topping; sprinkle evenly over bread. Bake in a 375° F. oven for 30 minutes, or until lightly browned.

Makes 8 to 10 servings.

Oatmeal Raisin Bread

SENSITIVITY CHECKLIST:

This recipe is   _____-free
    dairy

    _____-free
    egg

    _____-free
    wheat

    _____-free
    corn

    __✓-free
    sugar

If child has been placed on a natural salicylate-free diet, eliminate the raisins in this recipe and substitute grated lemon peel for the orange rind in the ingredients. Although the recipe is free of refined sugar, it does contain corn syrup as a sweetener and flavoring agent, about 1 teaspoon per slice.

1½ cups boiling water
1 cup quick oats cereal
½ cup light corn syrup
⅓ cup butter
1 tablespoon salt
2 packages active dry yeast
½ cup warm water
2 eggs, slightly beaten
2 cups raisins
2 tablespoons grated orange rind
½ teaspoon allspice
6 to 6¼ cups sifted flour

Mix boiling water, oats, corn syrup, butter, and salt in a large bowl. Stir until butter is melted, then cool to lukewarm. Sprinkle yeast into the ½ cup warm water and stir until dissolved. Add the yeast mixture, eggs, raisins, orange rind, and allspice to the oats mixture. Vigorously stir in flour, 1 cup at a time, until a smooth, moist dough forms. Cover; chill 1½ to 2 hours. Grease two 1½- to 2-quart round casseroles; set aside. Place chilled dough on a lightly floured board. With greased hands, shape (do not knead) into round loaves and place in prepared casseroles. Cover and let rise in a warm place, free from drafts, just until doubled in bulk, 50 to 60 minutes. The dough will be about even with the tops of the casseroles. Bake in a preheated 350° F. oven for 50 to 60 minutes or until bread is browned. Remove from casseroles and cool on wire racks.

Makes 2 loaves.

Irish Soda Bread

SENSITIVITY CHECKLIST:

This recipe is ＿＿-free (dairy)

✓-free (egg)

＿＿-free (wheat)

✓-free (corn)

＿＿-free (sugar)

Here's another quick-mixing egg-free bread. If you have a heavy black iron skillet, use it to bake this bread.

2 cups all-purpose flour
1½ teaspoons baking powder
¼ teaspoon baking soda
1 teaspoon salt
3 tablespoons sugar
1 cup buttermilk

Mix flour, baking powder, baking soda, salt, and sugar together. Stir in buttermilk to make a soft dough. Knead dough on a lightly floured board for about a minute; then shape it into a round loaf and put it into an 8-inch greased round pan. Pat flour lightly over the top surface, then cut crosswise into the top. Bake in a preheated 350° F. oven for 40 minutes, or until done. Bread should have a hollow sound when you tap it.

Makes 8 servings.

Buttermilk Bran Bread

SENSITIVITY CHECKLIST:

This recipe is ⬜ _____-free   *dairy*

✔ -free   *egg*

_____-free   *wheat*

✔ -free   *corn*

_____-free   *sugar*

This is such an easy nourishing bread, you'll wonder why you didn't discover breadmaking long ago. Freezes well too.

1⅔ cups crushed whole-bran cereal
4⅓ cups sifted flour
1 tablespoon baking soda
1 teaspoon sugar
1 teaspoon salt
2½ cups buttermilk

Preheat oven to 350° F. Mix together cereal, flour, baking soda, sugar, and salt. Make a well in the center and pour in buttermilk. Work quickly and knead dough lightly; shape into a loaf and press into a greased 9-by-5-inch loaf pan. Bake 1 hour, or until firm and lightly browned.

Makes 1 loaf.

Pumpkin Bread

SENSITIVITY CHECKLIST:

This recipe is   **dairy**   ✔-free

    egg   ____-free

    wheat   ____-free

    corn   ✔-free

    sugar   ____-free

If child has been placed on a sugar-free diet, omit this recipe. If child has been placed on a natural salicylate-free diet, omit orange, raisins, and dates. Substitute ½ grapefruit for the orange and increase the amount of nuts. It's a very delicious batter bread that goes into the oven with a minimum of fuss.

⅔ cup pure vegetable shortening
2⅔ cups sugar
4 eggs
1 can (1 pound) pumpkin
⅔ cup water
3⅓ cups flour
2 teaspoons baking soda
1½ teaspoons salt
1 teaspoon cinnamon
½ teaspoon baking powder
1 orange (or ½ grapefruit)
⅔ cup chopped nuts
⅔ cup chopped raisins or dates

Cream shortening and sugar thoroughly. Add eggs, beating well. Add pumpkin and water. Sift together flour, baking soda, salt, cinnamon, and baking powder; add to pumpkin mixture. Remove seeds from orange after cutting it into sections (do not remove rind). Using a food processor, blender, or grinder, grind orange and rind; add to pumpkin mixture. Stir in nuts and raisins. Pour into two well-greased 9-by-5-inch loaf pans and bake in a 350° F. oven for 1 hour.

Makes 2 loaves.

———

NOTE: Second loaf may be frozen for future use.

Peanut Bread

SENSITIVITY CHECKLIST:

This recipe is  _____-free
dairy

_____-free
egg

_____-free
wheat

✓-free
corn

_____-free
sugar

If child is placed on a sugar-free diet, omit this recipe. Chunk-style peanut butter gives it an interesting texture. Always check labels on peanut butter to determine that it is free from artificial additives.

½ cup creamy or chunk-style peanut butter
¼ cup butter
2 cups sifted flour
2½ teaspoons baking powder
1 teaspoon salt
½ cup light brown sugar
2 teaspoons grated lemon rind
1 egg, slightly beaten
1 cup milk

Grease an 8½-by-4½-by-2½-inch loaf pan. Mix peanut butter and butter until light and fluffy. Sift together flour, baking powder, and salt; stir in sugar. Add to peanut butter mixture, working in with spoon or fork until fine crumbs form. Add lemon rind. Mix egg and milk. Add to flour mixture and stir just until moistened. Turn batter into prepared pan. Bake in a 350° F. oven about 60 minutes or until a cake tester inserted in center comes out clean. Cool bread in pan 10 mintues. Remove from pan and cool completely on wire rack.

Makes 1 loaf.

————

NOTE: Bread slices best on second day. Wrap with foil or plastic wrap overnight.

Carrot Peanut Bread

SENSITIVITY CHECKLIST:

This recipe is  _____-free
dairy

_____-free
egg

_____-free
wheat

✓-free
corn

_____-free
sugar

If child has been placed on a sugar-free diet, omit this recipe. If there is no corn sensitivity, corn oil may be used for salad oil.

1 cup dark brown sugar
½ cup creamy peanut butter
½ cup salad oil
2 eggs
2 cups finely shredded carrot
1¾ cups unsifted flour
1 teaspoon baking powder
1 teaspoon baking soda
½ teaspoon salt
1 teaspoon ground cinnamon
1 teaspoon ground nutmeg
½ cup milk
1 teaspoon pure vanilla extract

Grease a 9-by-5-by-3-inch loaf pan. In a large bowl of electric mixer mix together brown sugar, peanut butter, oil, and eggs until creamy. Add carrot. In small bowl stir together flour, baking powder, baking soda, salt, cinnamon, and nutmeg. Stir together milk and vanilla. Add flour mixture to peanut butter mixture alternately with milk in three additions beginning and ending with flour. Turn into prepared pan. Bake in a 350° F. oven 1 hour or until cake tester inserted in center comes out clean. Cool 10 minutes; remove from pan.

Makes 1 loaf.

NOTE: To make Carrot Peanut Muffins follow recipe for Carrot Peanut Bread. Turn batter into 18 greased 2½-by-1¼-inch muffin cups. Bake in a 350° F. oven 25 minutes. Makes 18 muffins.

Date and Walnut Loaf

SENSITIVITY CHECKLIST:

This recipe is   **✓**-free
dairy

_____-free
egg

_____-free
wheat

_____-free
corn

_____-free
sugar

If child has been placed on a natural salicylate-free diet, omit dates and increase walnuts to 1 cup. If child is sensitive to corn, omit cornstarch and increase flour to 3 cups; substitute other vegetable oil for corn oil. This is one of the batter breads that can easily be called a cake.

2½ cups sifted flour
¾ cup sugar
½ cup cornstarch
1 teaspoon salt
½ cup chopped walnuts
1 cup chopped dates
2 tablespoons corn oil
1 egg
2 teaspoons baking soda
1 cup boiling water

Grease a 9-by-5-by-3-inch loaf pan. Sift flour, sugar, cornstarch and salt together. Stir in walnuts and dates until dates are separated and coated. Beat corn oil and egg together until blended; stir into dry ingredients. Dissolve baking soda in boiling water and stir into flour mixture. Beat until well blended. Pour into prepared pan. Set in warm place free from draft for 10 minutes, to rise slightly. Bake in a 350° F. oven about 1 hour, or until cake tester inserted in center comes out clean. Serve with butter or cream cheese, if desired.

Makes 1 loaf.

Banana Bread

SENSITIVITY CHECKLIST:

This recipe is   **dairy** ____-free

   egg ____-free

   wheat ____-free

   corn __✓-free

   sugar ____-free

This is a lovely textured tea bread that can do double duty as a loaf for sandwiches or as a plain dessert cake. Either way, the whole family will think it's great. If child is not sensitive to corn, use corn oil for salad oil.

3 cups sifted flour
3½ teaspoons baking powder
1 teaspoon salt
½ cup chopped walnuts
¾ cup sugar
¼ cup salad oil
1 egg
⅔ cup milk
1 cup mashed ripe bananas

Sift together flour, baking powder, and salt. Mix nuts with 2 tablespoons of the dry ingredients. Mix sugar, salad oil, and egg in a large bowl until smooth. Stir in milk, then stir the dry ingredients. Stir in mashed bananas, then nuts. Turn into a greased and floured 9-by-5-by-3-inch loaf pan. Bake in a preheated 350° F. oven for about 1 hour and 15 minutes or until a wooden toothpick inserted in the center of loaf comes out clean. Cool in the pan 15 minutes; remove from pan and cool completely on a wire rack. Cut into thin slices to serve.

Makes 1 loaf.

Wheat-free Banana Bread

SENSITIVITY CHECKLIST:

This recipe is ____-free (dairy)

____-free (egg)

✓-free (wheat)

____-free (corn)

____-free (sugar)

Rice flour can be purchased at most health food stores. Think of this recipe whenever you have an overripe banana. Add a cup of broken walnuts to the batter for a change of texture.

1 cup rice flour
1 tablespoon baking powder
½ teaspoon salt
¼ cup butter, softened
¼ cup sugar
2 eggs, separated
½ cup milk
1 ripe banana, mashed

Preheat oven to 325° F. Sift together rice flour, baking powder, and salt; set aside. Cream butter; add sugar and beat until well blended. Beat in egg yolks. Add flour mixture alternately with milk, beating after each addition; add mashed banana. Beat egg whites until stiff peaks form and fold batter into egg whites. Spoon into a 9-by-5-by-3-inch greased loaf pan and bake 45 minutes. Cool before slicing.

Makes 1 loaf.

Wheat-free Corn Bread

SENSITIVITY CHECKLIST:

This recipe is  _✓_-free

_____-free

_✓_-free

_____-free

_____-free

This is such an easy bread to stir and bake that you may want to double it and make two at a time. One for dinner and one for the freezer.

2 cups corn flour
3 tablespoons baking powder
2 tablespoons sugar
½ teaspoon salt
3 eggs, slightly beaten
½ cup water
2 teaspoons corn oil

Preheat oven to 350° F. Sift together corn flour, baking powder, sugar, and salt. Add eggs, water, and oil and beat thoroughly. Pour into a greased loaf pan and bake 40 minutes, or until lightly browned.

Makes 1 loaf.

Corn Bread Squares

SENSITIVITY CHECKLIST:

This recipe is ____-free (dairy)

____-free (egg)

____-free (wheat)

____-free (corn)

____-free (sugar)

You won't miss a commercial mix when you whip up this corn bread. Use it for stuffing too. Omit if child is sensitive to dairy, egg, wheat, corn, or sugar.

1 cup unsifted flour
¾ cup corn meal
2 tablespoons sugar
2½ teaspoons baking powder
1 teaspoon salt
1 egg, well beaten
1¼ cups milk
¼ cup corn oil

Grease a 15½-by-10½-by-1-inch jelly.roll pan. Stir together flour, corn meal, sugar, baking powder, and salt. Mix together egg, milk, and corn oil. Add to flour mixture, mixing until dry ingredients are moistened (batter will be lumpy). Pour into prepared pan. Bake in a 425° F. oven 15 minutes or until lightly browned. Cool.

Makes 35 2-inch squares.

Yorkshire Pudding

SENSITIVITY CHECKLIST:

This recipe is ____-free (dairy)

____-free (egg)

____-free (wheat)

____-free (corn)

✔-free (sugar)

This takes the place of a bread when you are serving roasted meat. Whip it up when you remove the roast from the oven to let it rest before carving. It's best served hot from the oven, although batter may be prepared ahead of time and refrigerated until ready to use.

1 cup sifted flour
½ cup cornstarch
½ teaspoon salt
2 eggs, slightly beaten
1¾ cups milk
¼ cup hot meat drippings

Sift flour, cornstarch, and salt into mixing bowl. Stir in eggs, then gradually add 1 cup milk, mixing until smooth. Beat gently until slightly foamy on surface. Stir in remaining ¾ cup milk. Pour hot drippings into a 13-by-9-by-2-inch baking pan. Pour in batter. Bake in a 450° F. oven 10 minutes. Set oven temperature control at 350° F. and continue baking until mixture is golden brown and slightly firm on top, 25 to 30 minutes. Serve immediately.

Makes 6 servings.

Hamburger Buns

SENSITIVITY CHECKLIST:

This recipe is ⬚ _____-free
dairy

✓-free
egg

_____-free
wheat

✓-free
corn

_____-free
sugar

Try a yeast bread first to get the feel of rising dough. Then be brave and make your own hamburger buns. You'll know exactly what goes into them!

5¾ to 6¾ cups unsifted flour
⅓ cup instant nonfat dry milk solids
¼ cup sugar
½ teaspoon salt
2 packages active dry yeast
⅓ cup softened butter
2 cups warm water

In a large bowl thoroughly mix 2 cups of the flour, dry milk solids, sugar, salt, and undissolved yeast. Add butter. Gradually add warm water to dry ingredients and beat 2 minutes at medium speed of an electric mixer, scraping bowl occasionally. Add ¾ cup flour. Beat at high speed 2 minutes, scraping bowl occasionally. Stir in enough additional flour to make a stiff dough. Turn out onto a lightly floured breadboard; knead until smooth and elastic (about 8 to 10 minutes). Place in a bowl that has been greased with butter, turning to grease all sides. Cover; let rise in a warm place, free from drafts, until doubled in size, about 45 minutes. Punch dough down; let rise again until less than doubled, about 20 minutes. Divide dough in half; cut each half into 10 equal pieces. Form each piece into a smooth round ball. Grease baking sheets with butter and place the buns on them about 2 inches apart; press to flatten. Cover; let rise in a warm place, free from drafts, until doubled in size, about 1 hour. Bake in a 375° F. oven for 15 to 20 minutes or until done. Remove from baking sheets and cool on wire racks. Extra buns may be frozen for future use. Makes 20 buns.

Biscuits

This recipe is   _____ -free

dairy

✓ -free

egg

_____ -free

wheat

✓ -free

corn

✓ -free

sugar

Here's the easy way out of an egg-free and sugar-free bread problem—bake fresh and hot biscuits. It's such a loving thing to do.

2 cups sifted flour
3 teaspoons baking powder
1 teaspoon salt
4 tablespoons butter
⅔ cup milk

Sift flour, baking powder, and salt together. Cut in butter. Add milk to make a soft dough. Turn out on a floured board and knead for half a minute. Then roll out to ½-inch thickness and cut with a floured biscuit cutter. Bake on an ungreased baking sheet in a 450° F. oven for 10 to 12 minutes.

Makes 1 dozen.

Buttermilk Biscuits

SENSITIVITY CHECKLIST:

This recipe is  _____-free

dairy

✔-free

egg

_____-free

wheat

✔-free

corn

✔-free

sugar

Here's an old-fashioned recipe for Buttermilk Biscuits that puff up feather light. When you're in a hurry, just pat into a rectangle and cut in squares, then bake as indicated below.

2 cups sifted flour
1 tablespoon baking powder
1 teaspoon salt
¼ teaspoon baking soda
⅓ cup salad oil
⅔ cup buttermilk

Stir together flour, baking powder, salt, and baking soda. Blend in oil with a fork. Stir in buttermilk; mix until dough forms. Gently knead dough on a lightly floured board. Roll or pat out to a ½-inch thickness. Cut with a floured biscuit cutter or the floured rim of a glass and place on an ungreased cookie sheet. Bake in a preheated 450° F. oven for 12 to 15 minutes or until lightly browned.

Makes 12 biscuits.

———

NOTE: If you like soft-edged biscuits, place them close together on the cookie sheet. If you prefer them crusty, place farther apart.

Drop Biscuits

This recipe is ____-free

✓-free

____-free

____-free

✓-free

These biscuits don't even have to be rolled or patted into shape–just drop by spoonfuls. If child is sensitive to corn, another type of salad oil may be substituted.

2 cups sifted flour
1 tablespoon baking powder
1 teaspoon salt
½ cup corn oil
¾ cup milk

Sift together flour, baking powder, and salt. Blend in corn oil with a fork. Add milk and mix until dough forms. Drop dough by spoonfuls onto an ungreased cookie sheet. Bake in a preheated 450° F. oven for 12 to 15 minutes or until lightly browned.

Makes 12 biscuits.

Oatmeal Muffins

This recipe is   _____-free   *dairy*

_____-free   *egg*

_____-free   *wheat*

✓-free   *corn*

_____-free   *sugar*

This makes a good after-school snack and is easy to make and bake. Each has about 2 teaspoons of sugar.

1 cup raw oatmeal
½ cup light brown sugar
1 cup buttermilk
1 egg, beaten
¼ cup salad oil
1 cup sifted flour
2 teaspoons baking powder
½ teaspoon baking soda
½ teaspoon salt
¼ teaspoon cinnamon

Preheat oven to 375° F. Combine oatmeal and brown sugar; add buttermilk and stir well. Stir together egg and salad oil; add to oatmeal mixture. Sift together flour, baking powder, baking soda, salt, and cinnamon; stir into oatmeal mixture, just until all ingredients are moistened. Spoon mixture into a greased and floured muffin tin, filling ⅔ full. Bake for 25 minutes, or until lightly browned.

Makes 1 dozen muffins.

Blueberry-Rice Muffins

SENSITIVITY CHECKLIST:

This recipe is   _____-free   *dairy*

   __✓__-free   *egg*

   __✓__-free   *wheat*

   __✓__-free   *corn*

   _____-free   *sugar*

Here's a muffin that is both wheat-free and corn-free. For a different flavor you may substitute any kind of nuts (except almonds if child is placed on a natural salicylate-free diet) for blueberries.

1½ cups rice flour
⅔ cup hot water
2 tablespoons butter
¼ cup sugar
3 tablespoons baking powder
¼ teaspoon salt
1 teaspoon vanilla
1 teaspoon grated lemon rind
½ cup fresh blueberries, washed, stems removed

Preheat oven to 375° F. Combine half the flour with hot water; set aside. Cream together butter and sugar; add flour mixture and beat well. Stir together remaining flour, baking powder, and salt, and add flour mixture, vanilla, and grated lemon rind to batter. Stir in blueberries. Spoon into a greased muffin tin and bake 20 minutes.

Makes 8 muffins.

Rye Muffins

This recipe is   _____-free   *dairy*

_____-free   *egg*

_____-free   *wheat*

✔-free   *corn*

_____-free   *sugar*

If you want the taste of homemade rye bread but don't want to fuss with yeast dough, try these muffins. They bake in 25 minutes and have only one teaspoon of sugar each.

**1 cup flour
1 cup rye flour
4 teaspoons baking powder
¼ cup sugar
1 teaspoon salt
1 teaspoon caraway seeds
1 cup milk
1 egg**

Sift regular flour, rye flour, baking powder, sugar, and salt together; stir to distribute ingredients evenly. Add caraway seeds. Beat milk and egg together; add to dry ingredients. Beat well. Pour batter into greased muffin tins and bake at 350° F. for 25 minutes, or until lightly browned.

Makes 12 muffins.

Corn Muffins

SENSITIVITY CHECKLIST:

This recipe is ____-free *(dairy)*

____-free *(egg)*

_✓_-free *(wheat)*

__ _-free *(corn)*

____-free *(sugar)*

These corn muffins have about one teaspoon of sugar each, in case you're keeping track of sugar intake. Check with your doctor to see how much is allowed. If none is allowed omit recipe.

4 tablespoons butter
¼ cup sugar
2 eggs, separated
1 cup milk
1 cup corn meal
1 cup corn flour
4 teaspoons baking powder
½ teaspoon salt

Cream the butter and sugar together. Beat in egg yolks. Add milk. Sift corn meal, corn flour, baking powder, and salt together. Beat egg whites until stiff. Add dry ingredients to the egg yolk batter, stirring well. Then fold in the beaten egg whites. Spoon into greased muffin tins. Bake in a 350° F. oven for 25 minutes.

Makes 12 muffins.

Peanut Butter Muffins

This recipe is _____-free

_____-free

_____-free

__✓-free

_____-free

Again, this recipe takes advantage of children's enjoyment of high-protein peanut butter (check label to be sure there are no artificial additives). If child is not sensitive to corn, corn oil may be used where indicated. Omit recipe if child is sensitive to sugar.

1 cup dark brown sugar
½ cup creamy peanut butter
½ cup salad oil
2 eggs
1¾ cups unsifted flour
1 teaspoon baking powder
1 teaspoon baking soda
½ teaspoon salt
1 teaspoon ground cinnamon
1 teaspoon ground nutmeg
½ cup milk
1 teaspoon pure vanilla extract

Grease fourteen 2½-by-1¼-inch muffin cups. In large bowl of electric mixer mix together brown sugar, peanut butter, oil, and eggs until creamy. In small bowl stir together flour, baking powder, baking soda, salt, cinnamon, and nutmeg. Stir together milk and vanilla. Add flour mixture to peanut butter mixture alternately with milk in three additions beginning and ending with flour. Turn into prepared muffin cups. Bake in a 350° F. oven 25 minutes.

Makes 14 muffins.

Graham Muffins

SENSITIVITY CHECKLIST:

This recipe is   ____-free (dairy)

____-free (egg)

____-free (wheat)

__✓__-free (corn)

____-free (sugar)

These muffins freeze well, so you may want to double the recipe and store the leftovers in the freezer for future use. A good after-school snack with only a half-teaspoon of sugar each.

1 cup graham flour
1 cup regular flour
2 tablespoons sugar
4 teaspoons baking powder
½ teaspoon salt
1¼ cups milk
1 egg
4 tablespoons melted butter

Sift graham flour, regular flour, sugar, baking powder, and salt together; stir to distribute the ingredients evenly. Beat milk, egg, and melted butter together; stir into dry ingredients. Pour into greased muffin cups and bake in a 350° F. oven for 25 minutes, or until lightly browned.

Makes 12 muffins.

Pumpkin Muffins

SENSITIVITY CHECKLIST:

This recipe is  _____-free   *dairy*

_____-free   *egg*

_____-free   *wheat*

✓ -free   *corn*

_____-free   *sugar*

These muffins freeze well and are ideal to warm up for a special breakfast. It's a wonderful way to serve pumpkin. Each muffin contains 1½ teaspoons sugar.

3 cups sifted flour
¾ cup sugar
4 teaspoons baking powder
1½ teaspoons salt
1 teaspoon cinnamon
1 teaspoon nutmeg
2 eggs, beaten
1 cup milk
1 cup canned pumpkin
½ cup butter, melted and cooled

Sift together flour, sugar, baking powder, salt, cinnamon, and nutmeg into a large bowl. Combine eggs, milk, pumpkin, and butter; add to the dry ingredients. Stir until just well blended. Fill greased muffin cups two-thirds full. Bake in a preheated 400° F. oven for 15 to 18 minutes or until golden brown. Serve hot, with butter.

Makes 24 muffins.

Bread Crumbs

SENSITIVITY CHECKLIST:

This recipe is  _____-free

_____-free

_____-free

_____-free

_____-free

It's a shame to throw away good bread just because it is no longer soft enough to chew. Here's the way to make your own bread crumbs from it. Don't overlook making croutons too–just dice the bread evenly and bake as indicated below.

Stale bread
Dried parsley, optional
Grated Parmesan cheese, optional

Dice stale bread into small pieces and spread on a flat pan. Place in a 250° F. oven until bread is lightly browned. Process a few pieces at a time in a blender or food processor until all are in crumbs. Add parsley or grated Parmesan cheese, or both, just before using, if desired. Keep in a tightly closed container in a kitchen cupboard.

14

Desserts

If you are used to reaching for a packaged mix to bake a cake, or an artificially colored and flavored gelatin that stirs up into a quick dessert, or an instant pudding mix that can be whipped and served in minutes you'll have a lot of shopping homework to do. Those mixes may not be served to the hyperactive child if they have artificial additives—and most of them do.

Start-from-scratch cakes are easy enough to beat together if you have at least an electric hand beater and preferably a good sturdy machine that will stay anchored firmly to the counter. Keep your baking supplies together so it will be easy to assemble all the ingredients before starting. Always preheat the oven first so the proper temperature can be reached by the time you put the cake in the oven. Use recipes that have a minimum of sugar for the hyperactive child.

Gelatin desserts can be made by using unflavored gelatin and pure fruit juice. (If the child has been placed on a natural salicylate-free diet, do not use the juice of any fruit on that list. See chapter 3.) And as stated earlier, homemade popsicles may be made by freezing pure fruit juice in plastic forms with wooden sticks.

It's not so much what you serve sometimes as the way you present it.

Canned fruit (without heavy sugared syrup, and not natural salicylate fruit) is always a treat, and even more so when several kinds of fruit are mixed together. Top with a dab of pure whipped cream for special occasions. Just whip a little heavy sweet cream until it starts to thicken, form ripples, and then bursts into a fluffy appearance. (Don't beat an instant more or you're on your way to making butter.)

A fresh fruit bowl at the end of the dinner meal and for snacks in between is always in order, with some permitted fruit for the hyperactive child. If you can swing the whole family into reaching for a piece of fruit instead of cake or cookies, you'll be guiding them to a healthier way of eating.

If the child has proved sensitive to wheat, you may convert your regular flour-based recipes into gluten-free recipes by trying the following substitutions:

First, add 1 egg to the recipe if it contains less than 2 cups of regular flour. Then make these exchanges for each cup of regular flour in the recipe, choosing one that will have an appropriate flavor when baked:

1 cup corn flour
¾ cup coarse corn meal
1 scant cup fine corn meal
⅝ cup potato flour
⅞ cup rice flour
1 cup soybean flour plus ¼ cup potato flour

You'll find several excellent wheat-free recipes in this chapter as well. Perhaps if you use them and study the ingredients, you'll be able to rescue some of your favorite recipes as well.

There are several egg-free recipes and corn-free ones too. You'll find an excellent dairy-free pastry, and can make easy substitutions for butter in any recipe by using pure vegetable shortening in its place. Some recipes have been made with peanut butter to give extra protein instead of dairy fat, and extra flavor as well.

Chocolate Honey Cake

SENSITIVITY CHECKLIST:

This recipe is   _____-free   *dairy*

_____-free   *egg*

_____-free   *wheat*

__✓__-free   *corn*

__✓__-free   *sugar*

Use only pure baking chocolate for this recipe. Chopped nuts may be added to batter if desired. Sprinkle well with some of the flour mixture to spread nuts evenly through the batter. Omit recipe if child is sensitive to chocolate.

½ cup butter
1¼ cups honey
2 cups sifted cake flour
1½ teaspoons baking soda
½ teaspoon salt
2 eggs
3 squares unsweetened baking chocolate, melted
⅔ cup water
1 teaspoon pure vanilla extract

Beat butter until fluffy; add honey gradually and beat well. Sift flour, baking soda, and salt together. Add ½ cup flour mixture to butter mixture and beat well. Add eggs. Stir in melted chocolate. Add 1 cup flour mixture and beat well. Slowly add water. Add remaining flour mixture. Add vanilla. Pour into a greased 9-inch tube pan. Bake at 350° F. for 40 minutes, or until cake tests done. Cool before slicing.

Makes 16 servings.

Sour Cream Coffee Cake

SENSITIVITY CHECKLIST:

This recipe is  _____-free
dairy

_____-free
egg

_____-free
wheat

___✓-free
corn

_____-free
sugar

If child has been placed on a natural salicylate-free diet, omit raisins in the topping. There are about 4 teaspoons of sugar in each serving.

**½ pound butter
1 cup sugar
2 eggs
2 cups sifted flour
¼ teaspoon salt
1 teaspoon baking powder
1 teaspoon baking soda
1 cup dairy sour cream
1 teaspoon pure vanilla extract**

TOPPING

**1 teaspoon sugar
1 teaspoon cinnamon
¼ cup raisins
¼ cup chopped nuts**

Beat butter and sugar together until fluffy. Add eggs. Sift flour, salt, baking powder, and baking soda together; add to batter alternately with the sour cream. Add vanilla. Pour into a 7-by-11-inch buttered pan. Combine topping ingredients and sprinkle evenly over batter. Bake in a 350° F. oven for 30 minutes.

Makes 12 servings.

Cream Cheese Pound Cake

This recipe is ____-free (dairy)

____-free (egg)

____-free (wheat)

✓-free (corn)

____-free (sugar)

Once you have tasted this pound cake you may want to double the recipe and bake a second loaf for the freezer. It's a one-bowl cake that whips up in a few minutes.

1 package (3 ounces) pure cream cheese
½ cup butter
1 cup sugar
3 eggs
1 cup sifted cake flour
1 teaspoon pure vanilla extract
1 teaspoon freshly grated lemon rind

Beat the cheese and butter together. Add sugar and beat well. Add eggs one at a time. Add flour. Add vanilla and grated lemon rind. Pour into a buttered and floured 8½-by-4½-inch loaf pan. Bake in a preheated 350° F. oven for 50 to 60 minutes, or until lightly browned on top.

Makes 8 servings.

Applesauce Oatmeal Cake

SENSITIVITY CHECKLIST:

This recipe is ____-free (dairy)

____-free (egg)

____-free (wheat)

✔-free (corn)

____-free (sugar)

Make the applesauce yourself or check the label on the commercial variety to be sure that there are no artificial additives. Then enjoy this naturally wonderful cake.

2 cups applesauce
½ cup butter
1 cup quick oats
1 cup sugar
1 cup brown sugar
2 eggs, beaten
1 teaspoon pure vanilla extract
1½ cups flour
1 teaspoon baking soda
1 teaspoon cinnamon
⅛ teaspoon salt

Combine applesauce and butter in a saucepan. Heat until butter is melted, stirring constantly. Remove from heat and stir in oats; set aside Beat together sugar, brown sugar, eggs, and vanilla. Stir in oat mixture. Sift together flour, baking soda, cinnamon, and salt; add to mixture. Pour into a greased 11¾-by-7½-inch baking dish. Bake in 350°F. oven 35 to 40 minutes, or until lightly browned.

Makes 12 servings.

Peanut Butter Chocolate Cake

SENSITIVITY CHECKLIST:

This recipe is   _____-free
dairy

    ✔-free
egg

    _____-free
wheat

    ✔-free
corn

    _____-free
sugar

After checking ingredients to be sure that the peanut butter and choco-late are without additives, bake away. You'll give the whole family a combination that they'll enjoy. It's one of the rare no-egg cakes that is worth making. Omit recipe if child is sensitive to chocolate.

1¾ cups unsifted cake flour
1 cup sugar
¾ teaspoon salt
¾ teaspoon baking soda
¼ cup creamy or chunk-style peanut butter
2 tablespoons butter
2 unsweetened chocolate squares, 1 ounce each, melted
1 teaspoon pure vanilla extract
1 cup buttermilk or sour milk*

Grease two 8-by-1½-inch layer cake pans; line bottoms with waxed paper. Sift together flour, sugar, salt, and baking soda. Stir peanut butter and butter in mixing bowl until blended. Mix in chocolate and vanilla. Add flour mixture alternately with milk, beginning and ending with flour and mixing until smooth after each addition. Pour into pre-pared cake pans. Bake in 350° F. oven about 25 minutes or until cake tester inserted in center comes out clean.

Makes 1 layer cake.

NOTE: To make Peanut Butter Chocolate Cupcakes pour batter into eighteen 2½-by-1¼-inch cupcake pans lined with paper liners. Bake as directed for Peanut Butter Chocolate Cake. Makes 18 cupcakes.

* To make sour milk add 1 tablespoon lemon juice or vinegar to 1 cup whole milk.

Layer Cake Supreme

SENSITIVITY CHECKLIST:

This recipe is   _____-free *dairy.*

  _____-free *egg*

  _____-free *wheat*

  ✓ -free *corn*

  _____-free *sugar*

This cake freezes well, so consider wrapping one layer in aluminum foil and placing it in the freezer for future use. Frost as desired.

2 cups sifted cake flour
1 cup brown sugar
½ cup sugar
2 teaspoons baking powder
¼ teaspoon baking soda
1 teaspoon salt
⅓ cup butter
½ cup creamy or chunk style peanut butter
⅔ cup milk
2 eggs
⅓ cup milk
1 teaspoon pure vanilla extract

Sift flour, sugars, baking powder, baking soda, and salt together into mixing bowl. Add butter, peanut butter, and ⅔ cup milk. Stir until blended, then beat until batter is smooth. Add eggs, ⅓ cup milk, and vanilla. Beat until smooth and creamy. Pour into 2 well-greased 8-inch layer cake pans. Bake in 350° F. oven until cake tests done, about 35 minutes. (Insert toothpick. Done if comes out clean.)

Each layer makes 8 servings.

Peanut Butter Party Cake

SENSITIVITY CHECKLIST:

This recipe is   _____-free
dairy

_____-free
egg

_____-free
wheat

✓-free
corn

_____-free
sugar

Here's a cake for the birthday child that the parents will enjoy too. It has the texture of a sponge cake and the suggestion of peanut butter that most kids love. Frost as desired.

2½ cups sifted cake flour
2½ teaspoons baking powder
¼ teaspoon baking soda
½ teaspoon salt
¼ cup butter
¼ cup creamy peanut butter
1½ cups sugar
2 eggs, separated
1 teaspoon pure vanilla extract
1 cup milk

Grease a 13-by-9½-by-2-inch cake pan; line bottom with waxed paper. Sift flour, baking powder, baking soda, and salt together. Cream butter with peanut butter in large mixing bowl. Gradually add 1¼ cups sugar, beating until mixture is light and fluffy. Blend in egg yolks and vanilla. Add dry ingredients alternately with milk, beginning and ending with dry ingredients. Beat egg whites in small bowl until foamy. Gradually add ¼ cup sugar, beating until mixture forms soft peaks when beater is raised. Gently fold into batter. Pour into prepared cake pan. Bake in a 350° F. oven until cake tests done, 35 to 40 minutes. Cool thoroughly before frosting.

Makes 16 servings.

Cocoa Chiffon Cake

SENSITIVITY CHECKLIST:

This recipe is   dairy ___✓___-free

egg _____-free

wheat _____-free

corn __✓___-free

sugar _____-free

This dessert treat may be served topped with pure ice cream (no additives) if allowed by physician. Keep in mind that with 16 slices, each slice contains 4½ teaspoons of sugar. Omit recipe if child is sensitive to chocolate.

1½ cups sifted cake flour
1½ cups sugar
¼ cup pure cocoa
1 teaspoon baking soda
1 teaspoon salt
7 eggs, separated
½ cup salad oil
¾ cup water
1 teaspoon pure vanilla extract
½ teaspoon cream of tartar

Sift flour, ½ cup of the sugar, cocoa, baking soda, and salt into a small mixing bowl. Add egg yolks, oil, water, and vanilla. Beat at low speed until blended. Beat at medium speed until smooth, about 2 minutes. Beat egg whites until foamy; add cream of tartar and beat until soft peaks form. Gradually add the remaining 1 cup sugar, beating well after each addition. Fold in the egg yolk mixture. Pour batter into an ungreased 10-inch tube pan. Bake in a preheated 325° F. oven for 55 minutes. Increase temperature to 350° F. and bake an additional 10 minutes. Invert pan and let cool.

Makes 12 to 16 servings.

Wheat-free Sponge Cake

SENSITIVITY CHECKLIST:

This recipe is

dairy ___✓___-free

egg _____-free

wheat ___✓___-free

corn ___✓___-free

sugar _____-free

Yes, it's possible to eat cake when on a wheat-free diet. Each generous slice contains about 2 tablespoons of sugar, so if the child is on a sugar-restricted diet you might want to slice cake thinner, if this kind of special treat is permitted by doctor.

6 eggs, separated
1 whole egg
1½ cups sugar
2 tablespoons lemon juice
Grated rind of 1 lemon
1 cup sifted potato flour
½ teaspoon salt
½ teaspoon nutmeg
Confectioners' sugar (optional)

Preheat oven to 350° F. Beat egg yolks and whole egg together until foamy; beat in sugar and add lemon juice and rind. Sift together potato flour and salt; add to egg yolk batter with nutmeg. Beat egg whites until stiff and fold into the batter. Grease bottom of a 10-inch springform pan and pour batter into pan. Bake 35 minutes, or until cake is firm in center. Cool upside down before removing side of springform pan. Dust with confectioners' sugar, if desired.

Makes 12 servings.

Wheat-free Cupcakes

SENSITIVITY CHECKLIST:

This recipe is ⬚ ____-free
dairy

○ ____-free
egg

✔-free
wheat

____-free
corn

____-free
sugar

Use paper liners in the muffin tin and save a job of greasing and scrubbing it too. You'll find these paper liners in the baking goods section of your food market.

⅓ cup butter
⅓ cup sugar
1 egg
¼ teaspoon pure vanilla extract
1 cup sifted cornstarch
1 teaspoon baking powder
3 tablespoons milk

Preheat oven to 375° F. Cream butter and sugar; add egg and vanilla. Sift together cornstarch and baking powder and add alternately with milk. Spoon batter into greased muffin tin, filling ⅔ full. Bake 12 to 15 minutes, or until an inserted toothpick comes out clean.

Makes 8 cupcakes.

Dairy-free Pastry

SENSITIVITY CHECKLIST:

This recipe is

Check the label on the vegetable shortening to be sure that it does not contain any artificial coloring or flavoring agents. In addition, if there is a sensitivity to corn, be sure that it is not one of the ingredients in the vegetable shortening.

2 cups flour
1 teaspoon salt
⅔ cup pure vegetable shortening
4 to 5 tablespoons cold water

Mix flour, salt, and shortening together, using a pastry blender or two forks, until it looks like coarse corn meal. Slowly pour water over and work in. Refrigerate at least one hour. Then roll half the dough into a crust, using a floured board and floured rolling pin. Roll other half into second crust. Place one crust in pie pan, fill with desired filling and top with remaining crust. Crimp edges together to seal. If making a one-crust pie shell, place second crust in another pan and freeze until needed; or halve the recipe and prepare only one crust.

Makes 2 crusts.

Cream Cheese Pastry

SENSITIVITY CHECKLIST:

This recipe is   _____-free   **dairy**

     ✔-free   **egg**

     _____-free   **wheat**

     ✔-free   **corn**

     ✔-free   **sugar**

This pastry rolls out with great ease if you chill it first as directed. Fill with apples or other desired fruit, or use as a single crust for a homemade custard filling.

1 package (3 ounces) pure cream cheese
½ cup butter
1 cup flour

Let cream cheese and butter come to room temperature. Combine them and add flour. Knead into a smooth dough. Chill for several hours. When ready to use, roll out two crusts. Place one crust in pie pan, fill with desired filling and top with remaining crust. Crimp edges together to seal. If making a one-crust pie shell, place second crust in another pan and freeze until needed; or halve the recipe and prepare only one crust.

Makes 2 crusts.

Cherry Pie

SENSITIVITY CHECKLIST:

This recipe is dairy   ✔-free

egg   ✔-free

wheat   ____-free

corn   ✔-free

sugar   ____-free

If child has been placed on a natural salicylate-free diet, omit this recipe until permission has been granted to resume the use of cherries. If orange juice is permitted, try adding a few tablespoons to the pie crust before rolling out—it creates an unusual flavor.

2 prepared 9-inch pie crusts (see Index)
2 cups fresh sour cherries, pitted
2 tablespoons quick-cooking tapioca
1 tablespoon lemon juice
½ cup sugar
½ teaspoon cinnamon

Place first crust in pie pan. Combine cherries, tapioca, lemon juice, sugar, and cinnamon; mix gently but thoroughly. Let stand for ten minutes. Fill pie shell and cover with second crust. Prick top crust with a fork to let steam escape. Brush top crust with milk if desired. Bake in a 350° F. oven for 45 minutes, or until crust is lightly browned.

Makes 6 to 8 servings.

Apple Pie

SENSITIVITY CHECKLIST:

This recipe is  _____-free
dairy

✓-free
egg

_____-free
wheat

✓-free
corn

_____-free
sugar

If child has been placed on a natural salicylate-free diet, omit this recipe until permission has been granted to resume the use of apples. Each serving contains 1 tablespoon of sugar.

2 prepared pie crusts (see Index)
2 pounds tart apples, peeled and sliced
½ cup sugar
2 tablespoons flour
½ teaspoon cinnamon
¼ teaspoon nutmeg
⅛ teaspoon salt
1 tablespoon lemon juice
1 tablespoon butter

Place one pie crust into a 9-inch pie pan. Combine sliced apples, sugar, flour, cinnamon, nutmeg, and salt. Fill crust with mixture. Sprinkle with lemon juice and dot with butter. Top with second crust and crimp edges together. Prick with a fork to provide holes for steam to escape. Brush with milk. Bake at 425° F. for about 40 minutes, or until lightly browned.

Makes 8 servings.

Vanilla Pudding

SENSITIVITY CHECKLIST:

This recipe is   _____-free   dairy

✓ -free   egg

✓ -free   wheat

_____-free   corn

_____-free   sugar

No need to give up puddings when you can make your own so easily. Add other pure flavoring extracts, if desired.

⅓ cup sugar
¼ cup cornstarch
⅛ teaspoon salt
2¾ cups milk
2 tablespoons butter
1 teaspoon vanilla extract

Combine sugar, cornstarch, salt, and milk in a large saucepan; mix until smooth. Cook over medium heat, stirring constantly, until mixture comes to a boil; boil 1 minute and remove from heat. Stir in butter and vanilla and pour into individual serving dishes. Chill.

Makes 6 servings.

Chocolate-Vanilla Parfaits

SENSITIVITY CHECKLIST:

This recipe is   _____-free

dairy

_____-free

egg

✔-free

wheat

✔-free

corn

_____-free

sugar

No need to fret over the loss of packaged puddings. Here's an easy way to put your electric blender to work on a start-from-scratch dessert. Omit recipe if child is sensitive to chocolate.

2 envelopes unflavored gelatin
1½ cups cold milk
1 cup boiling milk
2 eggs
⅓ cup plus ¼ cup sugar
⅛ teaspoon salt
2 teaspoons pure vanilla extract
6 ice cubes
3 tablespoons unsweetened pure cocoa

Sprinkle gelatin over ½ cup of the cold milk in an electric blender container. Add 1 cup boiling milk; cover and blend on high speed until gelatin is dissolved. Add eggs, the ⅓ cup sugar, salt, 1 teaspoon of the vanilla, and the remaining 1 cup cold milk. Cover and blend until smooth. While blender is running, add ice cubes, one at a time. Continue blending until ice is dissolved. Spoon half of the mixture (about 2 cups) from blender container into a bowl and stir in the remaining 1 teaspoon vanilla; set aside. Add the ¼ cup sugar and cocoa to the mixture remaining in the blender container; cover and blend until smooth. Layer chocolate and vanilla mixtures in tall glasses. Chill at least 2 hours or until set.

Makes 6 to 8 servings.

Orange Parfaits

SENSITIVITY CHECKLIST:

This recipe is   _____-free
dairy

   _____-free
egg

   ✓-free
wheat

   ✓-free
corn

   _____-free
sugar

If child has been placed on a natural salicylate-free diet, substitute frozen pure grapefruit juice for the orange juice.

2 envelopes unflavored gelatin
½ cup cold water
½ cup boiling water
2 eggs
⅔ cup sugar
⅛ teaspoon salt
1 can (6 ounces) frozen orange juice concentrate
1 cup heavy cream
6 ice cubes

Sprinkle gelatin over cold water in a blender container. Add boiling water; cover and blend on low speed until gelatin is dissolved. Add eggs, sugar, and salt; cover and blend until smooth. Add unthawed orange juice concentrate; cover and blend on high speed until dissolved. Add heavy cream and ice cubes, one at a time. Continue blending until ice is dissolved. Pour into parfait glasses. Chill 1 hour.

Makes 8 parfaits.

Chocolate-Banana Pudding

SENSITIVITY CHECKLIST:

This recipe is _____-free
dairy

✓-free
egg

✓-free
wheat

✓-free
corn

_____-free
sugar

Prepare pudding the night before if you want to have an after-school snack waiting. Check cocoa label to be sure it is pure. Omit recipe if child is sensitive to chocolate.

2 envelopes unflavored gelatin
½ cup cold water
1 cup boiling water
¼ cup sugar
2 tablespoons unsweetened cocoa
⅔ cup nonfat pure dry milk powder
2 ripe bananas, cut into pieces
1 teaspoon pure vanilla extract
12 ice cubes

Sprinkle gelatin over cold water in a blender container. Add boiling water; cover and blend on low speed until gelatin is dissolved. Add sugar, cocoa, and dry milk; cover and blend until smooth. Add bananas and vanilla; blend on high speed. While blender is running, add ice cubes, one at a time. Continue blending until ice is dissolved. Quickly pour mixture into dessert dishes. Chill 20 to 30 minutes or until set.

Makes 8 servings.

Custard Fruit Cup

SENSITIVITY CHECKLIST:

This recipe is   ____-free

dairy

____-free

egg

✔-free

wheat

✔-free

corn

____-free

sugar

This recipe is excellent with berries of all kinds. If child is placed on a natural salicylate-free diet, do not use any of the fruits on that list in chapter 3.

4 eggs
½ cup sugar
¼ teaspoon salt
2½ cups milk, scalded
1½ teaspoons pure vanilla extract
3 cups cut-up fresh fruit

Beat eggs; add sugar and salt. Gradually pour scalded milk into the egg mixture, stirring constantly. Cook in the top of a double boiler over simmering water, stirring constantly, until mixture coats a silver spoon. Stir in vanilla. Cool immediately. Cover with foil, plastic wrap, or waxed paper and refrigerate. To serve, put ½ cup fresh fruit in each dessert dish. Spoon ½ cup custard over fruit. Garnish with a few additional pieces of fresh fruit before serving.

Makes 6 servings.

Rice Cream with Honeyed Fig Topping

SENSITIVITY CHECKLIST:

This recipe is   ___-free   **dairy**

___-free   **egg**

✓-free   **wheat**

✓-free   **corn**

___-free   **sugar**

If you prepare rice for dinner with enough left over to make this dessert, you'll have a head start for after-school snacking the next day. Or serve as dessert for tomorrow's dinner, if child is not on a four-day rotary diet.

1 envelope unflavored gelatin
1½ cups milk
1 package (3 ounces) cream cheese, softened
2 eggs, separated
¼ cup sugar
1 cup cooked rice
1 teaspoon pure vanilla extract
Honeyed Fig Topping (recipe follows)

Soften gelatin in ½ cup of the milk; set aside. In a large saucepan, blend the remaining 1 cup milk with cream cheese. Beat egg yolks slightly and stir into the cream cheese mixture with half of the sugar. Stir in the gelatin mixture. Cook over low heat, stirring constantly, until mixture coats the spoon. Stir in rice and vanilla. Cool slightly. Beat egg whites until frothy; then gradually beat in the remaining sugar, beating until whites are stiff. Gently fold into the rice mixture. Turn into a 1-quart mold. Chill until firm. Unmold and cut into wedges; serve with Honeyed Fig Topping.

Makes 6 to 8 servings.

Honeyed Fig Topping

SENSITIVITY CHECKLIST:

This recipe is   ____✓____-free

1 cup dried figs
3 tablespoons lemon juice
2 tablespoons honey

Put dried figs through a food grinder. Mix with lemon juice and honey. Cover tightly and refrigerate about 24 hours or until fruit softens and flavors blend.

Makes 1¼ cups of topping.

Baked Rice Pudding

SENSITIVITY CHECKLIST:

This recipe is ____-free (dairy)

✔-free (egg)

✔-free (wheat)

✔-free (corn)

____-free (sugar)

Be sure to use regular rice in this recipe rather than the "instant" kind that has been processed. Add raisins if the child has not been placed on a natural salicylate-free diet.

½ cup white rice
1 quart milk
¼ cup sugar
⅛ teaspoon salt
1 teaspoon pure vanilla extract

Preheat oven to 325° F. Combine rice, milk, sugar, salt, and vanilla. Pour into a buttered casserole; cover. Bake about 2 hours, or until rice has softened. Remove cover and bake a few minutes longer. Serve with whipped cream, if desired.

Makes 8 servings.

15

Cookies and Candy

According to current medical thinking about the management of the hyperactive child, you've got to declare war on the boxes of "junkfood" cookies and artificially colored and flavored candies that children seem to clamor for. Keep them out of the house entirely, if you can convince all other members of the household to do so. If not, at least educate the child to understand that these are absolutely forbidden sweets. With the current trend towards eating more natural and wholesome foods, it may not be as difficult to control as you may think.

You'll find many natural foods cookies in your food market and in your health food store. If the child is permitted to have an occasional sweet, (and is not sensitive to chocolate) purchase pure milk chocolate—read the label carefully as many chocolate products are not even made of chocolate these days. Watch out for those lollipops, especially the red and yellow ones. (You'll find colored flavorings in children's medicines, cough drops, toothpaste, and mouthwashes too. Have a chat with your pharmacist to find out what products you can safely purchase.)

Set up an old-fashioned cookie jar that is filled with natural ingredient cookies that you buy or bake. Keep all permissible candy nearby. Make a rule as to how much and when these snacks may be had by the special child, and make sure that your rules are carried out.

Have popcorn, dried fruit, fresh fruit, pretzels, and nuts available for safe snacks that are sugar-free. Peanut brittles and Cracker Jacks are usually safe (read the label).

Set aside a few hours every couple of weeks to bake cookies with the child or to have a fun time of making your own candy. There are many cookie recipes in this chapter, often with peanut butter for extra protein and flavor, and a number of easy to make candies too. They should all provide you with many hours of fun with your child and the answer to your sweet tooth problems. This chapter should be used only if your doctor permits the child to have an occasional intake of sugar. There are 16 tablespoons of sugar in one level measuring cup.

Chewy Crisps

SENSITIVITY CHECKLIST:

This recipe is

dairy _____-free

egg ✔-free

wheat ✔-free

corn _____-free

sugar _____-free

Here's another quick cookie that makes use of pure peanut butter. There's less than two teaspoons of sugar in each.

1 cup creamy or chunk-style peanut butter
1 cup sugar
½ cup undiluted evaporated milk
4 teaspoons cornstarch

Mix together peanut butter, sugar, milk, and cornstarch. Drop by teaspoonfuls onto ungreased baking sheet. Bake in a 350° F. oven 12 to 15 minutes or until light golden brown. Cool 1 to 2 minutes before removing from baking sheet.

Makes 36 cookies.

Crisp Peanut Butter Cookies

SENSITIVITY CHECKLIST:

This recipe is   ____-free
dairy

   ____-free
egg

   ____-free
wheat

   ✓-free
corn

   ____-free
sugar

No need to buy packaged cookies. Here's an easy recipe that makes 6 dozen cookies. Get the children into the baking act and they'll enjoy it even more. Each cookie contains about 1½ teaspoons of sugar.

1 cup butter
1 cup creamy or chunk style peanut butter
1 cup sugar
1 cup brown sugar
2 eggs, beaten
1 teaspoon pure vanilla extract
2½ cups sifted flour
1 teaspoon baking powder
1 teaspoon baking soda
1 teaspoon salt

Stir together butter, peanut butter, and sugars until blended. Beat in eggs and vanilla. Sift together flour, baking powder, baking soda, and salt over sugar mixture. Stir until well blended. If necessary, chill dough until it can be easily handled. Shape into 1-inch balls. Place about 2-inches apart on greased baking sheet. Flatten with floured bottom of glass or with floured fork making crosswise pattern. Bake in 350° F. oven 12 to 15 minutes, or until lightly browned.

Makes 6 dozen (2-inch) cookies.

Brazil Nut Cookies

SENSITIVITY CHECKLIST:

This recipe is  _____-free

_____-free

_ _ _-free

_____-free

_____-free

Here's a fast crunchy cookie ball that the whole family will smile about. If child is sensitive to corn, substitute ½ cup of additional flour where indicated on the recipe. Each cookie has about one teaspoon of sugar.

1 cup sifted flour
½ cup cornstarch
¾ cup butter
½ cup sugar
1 egg white
1 cup chopped Brazil nuts

Sift flour and cornstarch together; set aside. Blend butter and sugar. Stir in egg white. Gradually mix in sifted dry ingredients. Add nuts. Shape into 1-inch balls and place on lightly greased baking sheet. Bake in 400° F. oven 15 minutes, or until lightly browned.

Makes 2 dozen cookies.

Lemon-filled Cookies

This recipe is   _____-free
dairy

_____-free
egg

_____-free
wheat

_____-free
corn

_____-free
sugar

If child is placed on a natural salicylate-free diet, substitute pure vanilla extract for the almond extract until such time as the use of almonds may be resumed. Each cookie has about ¼ teaspoon of sugar before sprinkling with additional confectioners' sugar.

¾ cup sifted flour
¾ cup cornstarch
2 teaspoons baking powder
2 eggs
1 teaspoon pure almond extract
⅓ cup sugar
½ cup butter
Lemon Filling (recipe follows)
Confectioners' sugar

Sift together flour, cornstarch, and baking powder. Beat eggs until light and fluffy. Beat in extract, sugar, and butter. Mixture will not be smooth. Add flour mixture, stirring until smooth. Drop by level measuring teaspoonfuls onto greased baking sheet. Bake in a 400° F. oven 5 to 6 minutes or until edges are slightly browned. Spread about ½ teaspoon Lemon Filling on flat side of 1 cookie; sandwich with second cookie. Sprinkle lightly with confectioners' sugar.

Makes about 3½ dozen filled cookies.

Lemon Filling

SENSITIVITY CHECKLIST:

This recipe is  _____-free

_____-free

✓ _____-free

✓ _____-free

_____-free

½ cup sugar
1 egg, well beaten
3 tablespoons lemon juice
2 tablespoons butter

Stir together sugar, egg, lemon juice, and butter in small saucepan. Without letting mixture boil, cook over medium-low heat, stirring constantly, about 5 minutes or until mixture thickens. Cool while preparing cookies. Mixture thickens more as it cools.

Makes ⅔ cup.

Brown-edged Cookies

SENSITIVITY CHECKLIST:

This recipe is ____-free
dairy

____-free
egg

____-free
wheat

____-free
corn

____-free
sugar

These are simple drop cookies that form a nice wafer. Each one contains less than ½ teaspoon of sugar. Check the label on the chocolate chips to be sure they are pure. Omit chocolate chips if child is sensitive to them.

1 cup cornstarch
½ cup flour
¼ teaspoon salt
½ cup butter
½ cup sugar
2 eggs
½ cup pure chocolate chips
½ cup chopped nuts
¼ cup butter, melted

Sift cornstarch, flour, and salt together; set aside. Blend butter and sugar; beat in eggs. Gradually stir in sifted dry ingredients. Mix in chocolate chips and nuts. Drop by scant teaspoonfuls onto greased baking sheet 2 inches apart. Brush with melted butter. Bake in a 375° F oven 10 to 12 minutes or until golden brown.

Makes about 5 dozen.

Egg-free Cookies

SENSITIVITY CHECKLIST:

This recipe is ⬚ _____-free
dairy

〇 __✓__-free
egg

🌾 _____-free
wheat

🌽 _____-free
corn

🥣 _____-free
sugar

The child who is sensitive to eggs will be glad to have these cookies. Each one has about ⅔ teaspoon of sugar. If you flour your hands it will be easier to shape the cookies.

1½ cups sifted flour
¾ cup cornstarch
¾ cup confectioners' sugar
1 cup plus 2 tablespoons butter

Sift flour, cornstarch, and confectioners' sugar together into a large mixing bowl. Blend butter into dry ingredients, mixing until soft dough forms. Chill, if needed, until firm enough to handle. Shape into 1-inch balls. Place on ungreased cookie sheet, about 1½ inches apart. Flatten balls with lightly floured fork. Bake in a 300° F. oven until edges of cookies are lightly browned, 20 to 25 minutes.

Makes about 4 dozen.

Dairy-free Wafers

SENSITIVITY CHECKLIST:

This recipe is   ✓-free
     dairy

     _____-free
     egg

     _____-free
     wheat

     _____-free
     corn

     _____-free
     sugar

No butter in this tender wafer, but it's a tasty morsel anyway. If child is sensitive to corn, flour may be substituted for the 2 tablespoons of cornstarch. Each wafer has ½ teaspoon of sugar.

½ cup flour
2 tablespoons cornstarch
⅛ teaspoon salt
2 egg whites
2 egg yolks, slightly beaten
½ cup sugar
¾ teaspoon pure vanilla extract

Sift flour, cornstarch, and salt together; set aside. Beat egg whites until soft peaks form when beaters are raised. Beat in egg yolks, then sugar. Blend in sifted dry ingredients. Stir in vanilla extract. Drop by teaspoonfuls onto greased baking sheet 2 inches apart. Bake in a 400° F. oven 8 to 10 minutes or until golden brown in center with a slightly darker brown edge.

Makes 4 dozen.

Coconut Peanut Bars

SENSITIVITY CHECKLIST:

This recipe is  ＿＿-free

＿＿-free

＿＿-free

＿✔-free

＿＿-free

These crunchy bars have about 1½ teaspoons of sugar each, before rolling in confectioners' sugar. Store in a tightly covered canister to keep moisture in. Check label on peanut butter or make your own.

1 cup sifted flour
1 teaspoon baking powder
¼ teaspoon salt
⅓ cup butter
½ cup creamy or chunk-style peanut butter
1 cup sugar
2 eggs
1 teaspoon pure vanilla extract
1 cup flaked coconut
Confectioners' sugar

Grease an 11-by-7-by-1½-inch baking pan. Sift together flour, baking powder, and salt. Mix together butter, peanut butter, and sugar until blended. Stir in eggs and vanilla, mixing well. Stir in flour mixture, then coconut; spread evenly in prepared pan. Bake in 350° F. oven 25 to 30 minutes or until top springs back when lightly touched. Cut into bars; roll in confectioners' sugar while warm.

Makes 32 bars.

NOTE: An 8-by-8-by-2-inch cake pan may be used. Bake 30 to 35 minutes or until top springs back when lightly touched. Cut into bars; if desired, roll in confectioners' sugar while warm. Makes 32 bars.

Quick Crullers

This recipe is ⬚ _____-free
dairy

○ _____-free
egg

🌾 _____-free
wheat

🌽 ✓-free
corn

🥣 _____-free
sugar

If there's no time to bake but there's a need of a fast snack, consider this trick of frying stuffed bread roll-ups. Use corn oil if there is no sensitivity to corn.

1 cup sifted flour
1 teaspoon baking powder
½ teaspoon salt
1 egg, slightly beaten
1 cup milk
8 slices thin sliced white bread (no artificial additives), crusts
removed
Creamy or chunk-style peanut butter
Flour
Cooking oil
Cinnamon sugar

Sift together flour, baking powder, and salt. Mix egg and milk; add to flour mixture and beat until smooth. Spread bread with peanut butter. Cut slices into quarters, lengthwise, roll up, and fasten with wooden picks. Pour oil into heavy deep fryer or deep skillet, filling utensil ⅓ full. Heat over medium heat to 375° F. Dust outside of rolls with a little flour, dip into batter, and drain off excess. Fry rolls in hot oil a few at a time, turning once, about 4 minutes or until browned on all sides. Drain on absorbent paper. Remove picks. Dust rolls with cinnamon sugar. Serve warm.

Makes 32 small crullers.

NOTE: If desired, spread a thin layer of pure jelly over peanut butter before rolling up.

Ladyfingers

This recipe is

dairy ✔-free

egg ____-free

wheat ____-free

corn ____-free

sugar ____-free

Most baked goods at the store have artificial additives, so if you need ladyfingers you may have to bake them yourself. They taste much better too.

6 eggs
1¼ cups sugar
1 teaspoon pure vanilla extract
1 cup sifted cake flour
⅓ cup cornstarch
¼ teaspoon salt

Grease and lightly flour ladyfinger pans. Beat together eggs, 1 cup of the sugar, and vanilla on medium-high speed of electric mixer until light and lemon colored and double in bulk. Sift together flour, cornstarch, and salt. Gradually fold into beaten egg mixture, mixing well. Fill each ladyfinger shape with about 2 tablespoons of batter. When all are filled, sprinkle with about 1 tablespoon of sugar per dozen ladyfingers. Keep remaining batter refrigerated while baking first batch. Bake in 350° F. oven, 12 to 15 minutes, or until cake tester inserted in center comes out clean. Cool slightly; remove from pan; cool on rack. Makes about 4 dozen ladyfingers.

Makes about 2 dozen.

NOTE: Recipe may be cut in half. Use 3 tablespoons cornstarch.

Macaroons

SENSITIVITY CHECKLIST:

This recipe is

dairy ___✔___-free

egg _____-free

wheat ___✔___-free

corn _____-free

sugar _____-free

This delicious cookie is made without dairy or wheat products, but if the child is placed on a natural salicylate-free diet do not use this recipe until permission has been granted to resume the use of almonds. Each cookie contains about 2 teaspoons of sugar.

1¼ cups ground blanched almonds
¾ cup sugar
2 egg whites
2 tablespoons cornstarch
2 teaspoons water
¼ teaspoon pure vanilla extract
18 to 20 blanched almond halves

Combine ground almonds and sugar. Add unbeaten egg whites, reserving about 1 tablespoon to brush on top of macaroons. Stir for 1 minute or until well blended. Add cornstarch, water, and vanilla, stirring well after each addition. Drop batter onto foil-covered baking sheet by teaspoonfuls 3 inches apart. Brush cookies with remaining egg white, then place almond half on top of each. Bake in 375° F. oven 15 minutes or until evenly browned. Cool on wire rack 3 to 4 minutes or until foil may be peeled off. Remove foil; cool cookies on wire rack.

Makes about 1½ dozen.

Coconut-Peanut Macaroons

SENSITIVITY CHECKLIST:

This recipe is  ___✔___-free dairy

___-free egg

___-free wheat

___✔___-free corn

___-free sugar

If child has been placed on a sugar-free diet omit this recipe. Each cookie contains 1⅓ teaspoons sugar. Use chunky peanut butter (remember to check label) if a more textured cookie is desired.

3 egg whites
1 cup sugar
1 tablespoon flour
½ cup creamy peanut butter
1 cup shredded coconut

Beat egg whites until foamy. Gradually add sugar and continue to beat until egg whites are stiff and thick. Fold in flour. Fold meringue into peanut butter. Fold in coconut. Drop by tablespoonfuls onto ungreased cookie sheet covered with brown paper. Bake in a 325° F. oven, 20 to 25 minutes. Remove from paper when cool.

Makes approximately 3 dozen macaroons.

Chocolate Peanut Butter Brownies

SENSITIVITY CHECKLIST:

This recipe is  _____-free
dairy

_____-free
egg

_____-free
wheat

✓-free
corn

_____-free
sugar

Be sure that the labels on the chocolate and peanut butter affirm that they are pure. The brown sugar gives a unique flavor. Each bar has one tablespoon of sugar. Omit recipe if child is sensitive to chocolate.

½ cup sifted flour
½ teaspoon baking powder
¼ teaspoon salt
4 tablespoons butter
¼ cup creamy or chunk-style peanut butter
2 squares (2 ounces) unsweetened chocolate
1 egg
1 cup brown sugar
1 teaspoon pure vanilla extract
½ cup chopped peanuts

Sift flour, baking powder, and salt together. Melt butter, peanut butter, and chocolate in saucepan over low heat. Stir until blended. Beat egg, then gradually add sugar, beating until well blended. Stir in peanut butter mixture and vanilla. Mix in sifted dry ingredients, then nuts. Turn into a greased 8-by-8-by-2-inch baking pan. Bake in a 350° F. oven about 30 minutes or until brownies test done. (Insert toothpick. Done if comes out clean.) Cut as desired.

Makes 16 squares, about 2 inches each.

———

NOTE: If salted peanuts are used, omit salt.

Peanut Oatmeal Brownies

SENSITIVITY CHECKLIST:

This recipe is   ____-free   *dairy*

____-free   *egg*

____-free   *wheat*

__✓__-free   *corn*

____-free   *sugar*

If child has been placed on a sugar-free diet, omit this recipe. If not, it makes a filling dessert or after-school snack. Each contains 2 teaspoons of sugar.

⅔ cup butter
⅔ cup creamy or chunk-style peanut butter
1½ cups light brown sugar
3 eggs
1½ cups unsifted flour
⅔ cup quick oats cereal, uncooked
2 teaspoons baking powder
½ teaspoon salt

Grease a 9-by-9-by-2-inch baking pan. Mix together butter and peanut butter on medium speed of mixer. Add brown sugar and beat well. Beat in eggs. Stir together flour, oatmeal, baking powder, and salt. Gradually add to peanut butter mixture and beat well. Turn into prepared pan. Bake in a 350° F. oven 40 to 50 minutes, or until cake tester inserted in center comes out clean.

Makes 36 squares.

Shortbread

SENSITIVITY CHECKLIST:

This recipe is   ____-free   *dairy*

✓-free   *egg*

____-free   *wheat*

____-free   *corn*

____-free   *sugar*

Here's another easy cookie dough that just gets patted into the pan. Each piece contains a mere ½ teaspoon of sugar.

2 cups sifted flour
1 cup cornstarch
Dash salt
1 cup butter
½ cup sugar

Sift flour, cornstarch, and salt together. Cream butter and ½ cup sugar until light and fluffy. Add dry ingredients gradually until dough is stiff enough to work with hands. Knead on lightly floured cloth or board until well blended and smooth. Press into a 12-by-8-inch rectangle on baking sheet. Smooth over top. Score almost through with knife into 1-by-2-inch rectangles; prick with fork. Bake in a 325° F. oven for 30 to 40 minutes or until golden brown. Recut rectangles and sprinkle with additional sugar while still hot. Cool completely; remove from baking sheet. Store in an airtight container.

Makes 4 dozen rectangles.

NOTE: For triangles divide 12-by-8-inch rectangle into 24 squares (2 inches each). Cut each square in half diagonally. Makes 4 dozen triangles.

Peanut Butter Candy

SENSITIVITY CHECKLIST:

This recipe is   ____-free   (dairy)

✔-free   (egg)

✔-free   (wheat)

____-free   (corn)

____-free   (sugar)

If you want to have control of the child's candy habits you may want to make the candy yourself. In this recipe most of the ingredients are nutritious as well as satisfying. Sweet stuff measures out to about 2 teaspoons per piece, depending on how much confectioners' sugar is used for the coating.

1 cup creamy or chunk-style peanut butter
1 cup light corn syrup
1¼ cups nonfat dry milk
½ cup sifted confectioners' sugar

Mix together peanut butter and corn syrup until blended. Add nonfat dry milk. Form into 1-inch balls and roll in confectioners' sugar. Chill, if desired.

Makes 50 balls.

Chocolate Peanut Candy

SENSITIVITY CHECKLIST:

This recipe is   ____-free
dairy

✓-free
egg

✓-free
wheat

✓-free
corn

____-free
sugar

If child is not on a sugar-free diet and is permitted a sweet once in a while, here's a good one to make with popular peanut butter. Check label of chocolate carefully before purchasing to be sure that no artificial additives are included. Omit recipe if child is sensitive to chocolate.

1½ tablespoons butter
3 (1 ounce each) squares pure semisweet chocolate
½ cup creamy or chunk-style peanut butter
½ cup confectioners' sugar

Melt butter and chocolate in top of double boiler over hot, not boiling, water. Stir occasionally until melted. Cool slightly. Mix peanut butter and sugar in small bowl. Form into 1-inch balls. Using two spoons, dip balls in chocolate and coat completely. Place on waxed paper. Set in cool place until firm. Store covered in refrigerator.

Makes about 1½ dozen candies.

Peanut Butter Popcorn Balls

SENSITIVITY CHECKLIST:

This recipe is

dairy ✔-free

egg ✔-free

wheat ✔-free

corn ____-free

sugar ____-free

Once in a while, if the child has permission to have an occasional sweet treat, these popcorn balls will be fun to make and eat. Each ball has the equivalent of 1 tablespoon of sugar, including the corn syrup.

½ cup light corn syrup
¼ cup sugar
½ cup creamy or chunk-style peanut butter
2 quarts freshly popped corn

Mix together corn syrup and sugar in a 1-quart saucepan. Cook over medium heat, stirring constantly, until mixture comes to boil and sugar is completely dissolved. Remove from heat. Stir in peanut butter until smooth. Immediately pour mixture over popped corn in large bowl. Stir until evenly coated. Grease hands and shape into 2-inch balls.

Makes 12 balls.

Peanut Brittle

SENSITIVITY CHECKLIST:

This recipe is ✔-free
dairy

✔-free
egg

✔-free
wheat

✔-free
corn

____-free
sugar

· *This is a simple way to make your own candy. The hyperactive child should not have free access to candy, but if some sweets are permitted this can be an occasion for fun while making it and a taste treat too.*

2 cups sugar
1 cup shelled unsalted peanuts

Butter a cookie sheet. Put sugar into a heavy skillet and cook over low heat until it slowly melts and turns into a clear reddish-brown colored liquid. Be careful not to let it burn. Meanwhile, arrange the peanuts in a single layer on the cookie sheet. Pour the melted sugar over them and allow it to harden. When cold and hard, break into pieces.

Makes about 1 pound.

Raisin Clusters

SENSITIVITY CHECKLIST:

This recipe is _✓_-free
dairy

_✓_-free
egg

_✓_-free
wheat

_____-free
corn

_____-free
sugar

If child has been placed on a natural salicylate-free diet, substitute any kind of nuts except almonds for the raisins, until permission has been granted to resume the use of grapes and raisins. Omit recipe if child is sensitive to chocolate.

1 package (6 ounces) semi-sweet pure chocolate chips
¼ cup light corn syrup
1½ teaspoons pure vanilla extract
2 tablespoons confectioners' sugar
2 cups raisins

Grease a cookie sheet. Combine chocolate chips and corn syrup in the top of a double boiler. Place over boiling water and stir until chocolate is melted. Mix in vanilla and confectioners' sugar. Mix in raisins. Drop by teaspoonfuls onto the cookie sheet. Chill until firm.

Makes about 3 dozen

Coconut Potato Kisses

SENSITIVITY CHECKLIST:

This recipe is _____-free (dairy)

✓-free (egg)

✓-free (wheat)

✓-free (corn)

_____-free (sugar)

Here's a way to turn leftover mashed potatoes into candy treats, if the doctor will allow your child to have them occasionally. They can be chocolate-coated by melting pure chocolate chips in the top of a double boiler and then dipping the cooled candy into the mixture to coat. If child is sensitive to chocolate, do not coat.

¾ cup warm mashed potatoes
1 tablespoon butter
Pinch of salt
1 teaspoon pure vanilla extract
1 pound confectioners' sugar
¾ pound shredded coconut

Cream together potato, butter, salt, and vanilla. Stir in the confectioners' sugar. Stir in shredded coconut. Drop by teaspoonful on waxed paper. Cool until set.

Makes about 3 dozen.

Index